CIVIL RIGHTS IN CANADA

CIVIL RIGHTS IN CANADA

(Self-Counsel Series)

by

P. Michael Bolton, B.A., LL.B.

(Cartoons by Matt McLean)

INTERNATIONAL SELF-COUNSEL PRESS LTD.

Vancouver   Toronto

ISBN 0 - 88908 - 000 - 3

Printed in Canada

First Edition   -- December, 1971
Second Edition -- December, 1972
Third Edition   -- August, 1973
Fourth Edition -- June, 1975

Self-Counsel Series is published by:

INTERNATIONAL SELF-COUNSEL PRESS LTD.

Head & Editorial Office
306 West 25th Street
North Vancouver, B.C.
Phone (604) 987-2412

Toronto Sales Office
Phone (416) 691-8116

Eastern Warehouse
R.R. #1,
Pefferlaw, Ontario.
Phone (705) 437-2565

CONTENTS

INTRODUCTION

The purpose of this volume is to provide sufficient information about our criminal procedures as will enable individuals who are not legally trained to know what their rights and duties are in the sphere of criminal law. It will primarily be useful to young persons who are involved in situations in which they may have difficulty with the police and other authorities. The most consistently replayed situations of this sort involve young people who appear "different," and who are stopped by police in the streets and checked for drugs or other contraband items. It will be useful also to those persons who are involved in political or other demonstrations over which the authorities keep a close guard.

Primarily because of the outmoded drug laws of this country, perhaps the majority of the population is in danger presently of having difficulty with the agencies of enforcement. The use of marihuana, hashish, and some other drugs is now so widespread that it affects persons in all spheres, groups, and echelons of Canadian society. For that reason this book gives fairly intensive treatment to the powers of the police under the Narcotic Control Act and under the Food and Drug Act. The powers of arrest, search, and seizure in these acts as well as the rights of citizens in dealing with police who stop, question, arrest, or attempt to search them under these acts, are discussed fully. There is also some discussion of the reaction of the courts to various types of situations in which charges of possession or trafficking are alleged.

On a broader scale, the whole spectrum of what happens to a person who is arrested and charged with an offence is considered, including the nature of the booking, fingerprinting, and photographing procedures, questioning by police, getting bail or being released on an interim basis before trial, aspects of the trial itself and of the nature of evidence and judicial decision-making.

The last four sections of the book, in the form of post-scripts, discuss the problems of what to do when police abuse their powers, the incongruity of Canadian law in allowing illegally obtained evidence to be used in criminal trials, and the matter of how to remedy police abuses by laying criminal charges or suing in civil law for damages.

Since the first edition of the book there have been a good many changes in the laws, the most important of which are as follows:

(a)   The new wiretap legislation is the most recent and it prohibits police from randomly wiretapping telephones of persons they are investigating. However, as will be seen in the new chapter dealing with this matter, there are some serious weaknesses in the legislation and once again the apparent protection of civil rights only masks and confuses the reality of the situation.

(b)   Another recent one is the creation of the conditional and absolute discharge sections in the Criminal Code. As the book indicates, the conditional discharge has been created primarily to deal with the situation where otherwise law-abiding citizens run into difficulty with the criminal law by using marihuana or hashish. The conditional discharge provides a political solution for the government by, on one hand, allowing it to maintain marihuana and hashish on the list of illegal drugs, while, on the other hand, allowing the courts to impose a conditional discharge -- a sort of conviction but one which doesn't technically qualify as a conviction. This is seen as another step in the direction started by the passing of the Prison Records Act which allowed persons with a summary offence to apply for a pardon from the offence two years after the date of the payment of the penalty.

(c)   The old vagrancy "A," "B," and "C" sections of the Criminal Code have now been repealed. Vagrancy "A," "B," and "C" used to include wandering, trespassing, street prostitution, and begging. Some of these things can still be caught, however, by other sections of the code that prohibit soliciting and the cause of a disturbance by impeding other persons. These still catch the street prostitutes and are discussed in the chapter under "Sex and the Law." However, it is clear that this has meant an improvement in the law because of the fact that the police can no longer stop persons without reason under the guise of the vagrancy law and demand that they give an explanation for their presence in the place where they are stopped. An explanation is no longer required and greater recognition has been given to the right of persons to remain silent when questioned by police officers.

(d)   The section dealing with the possession of instruments for the purpose of housebreaking has also been changed. Formerly a person who was in possession of a screwdriver or some such other instrument late at night could be charged and forced to give evidence on his or her own behalf to explain why he or she was in possession of the item charged. Now the police must have reasonable grounds for believing that the instrument has been or was about to be used for the purpose of housebreaking.

(e)   There has been a change in the situation of bail. The Bill of Rights gives the right to every person accused of a crime to have reasonable bail, which right is not to be denied without just cause. Formerly, this didn't mean much because once you were in custody, having been arrested and charged with an offence, it was up to you to satisfy the court that you were a strong member of the community with established roots and connections and that you would turn up for the trial. The effect of the new bail laws is to put the onus on the prosecutor to justify keeping the person in custody. Now the accused need not say anything when he or she appears in court for bail. The prosecutor must show cause or justify why the accused should be held in custody; otherwise, the accused must be released on bail.

Despite this recent advance, the Supreme Court of Canada has, in a recent case, revealed its desire to detract from the written word of the Canadian Bill of Rights. In this case, a person had been taken to a police station to take a breathalyzer. Before actually taking the test, he had heard the voice of his lawyer who had been called to the police station by his girlfriend. The accused's request to see his lawyer was refused and he was told he had no right to see his lawyer until after the test. He was threatened with a charge of refusing to take the test and, on the strength of this, did take the breathalyzer. In the Supreme Court of Canada it was argued that the results of the test were inadmissible because the evidence was obtained by violating the person's right to see a lawyer under the Bill of Rights. The majority of the Supreme Court of Canada ruled once again, as they had four years earlier in the case of **Regina v. Wray,** that illegally or improperly obtained evidence is still admissible if it is relevant. Even if the evidence is obtained illegally, the Supreme Court held there are still no grounds for excluding it if it is relevant. In doing this the court ignored the U.S. cases which exclude evidence obtained by violation of individual rights. The court rationalized this on the basis that the Constitution of the United States is fundamentally different from the Canadian Bill of Rights. And in particular it is different in the effect to be given to the due process of law provision in the Fourteenth Amendment for which -- the court held -- there was no counterpart in the British North America Act. It appears that the Supreme Court of Canada is making no progress at all toward giving effect to our Bill of Rights.

Perhaps the most substantial change in the criminal law is still yet to come. By this we mean softening of the laws against marihuana and hashish possession. This law is obviously outmoded, the public at large realize it, the law enforcement authorities realize it, and Parliament realizes it. The probable difficulty is that to repeal the laws would mean electoral death for the government responsible.

It is important to realize that from time to time the criminal laws do change, though never as rapidly as they have been changing in the last two years. The information in the book is a good guideline to what the law is at the present time. However, one should always be alert to the newspapers and other media regarding new or changed laws. This book will tell you what your rights are, what powers the police have, and what will happen to you if you run into difficulties and have a criminal charge laid against you. However, whenever you are charged with a criminal offence of any sort, be it a summary offence or an indictable offence, you are recommended to seek legal counsel. In Canada now there is no reason for a person to go to court on a criminal charge without a lawyer. There are legal aid offices in every province and you can always ask the court to appoint a legal aid lawyer if legal aid is denied by the legal aid office and if you do not have sufficient funds.

The purpose of this book is achieved if people who read it become more alert to their civil rights. Criminal law is an area of public law and it is an area of law about which everyone should be informed. It has traditionally been the province of police, judges, court clerks, lawyers, and so on. However, this situation was intolerable, especially in view of the fact that such vast numbers of people were starting to be affected by the criminal law and still are. More public consciousness about the laws can only be good.

CHAPTER I

WHAT TO DO WHEN STOPPED BY POLICE

The situations in which police have a lawful right to stop and question you are very limited in Canadian law. Police may stop any person whom they consider to be suspicious. A police officer is allowed to walk up to you in the street and ask you questions, just as any stranger can. There is no restriction whatever on an officer's right to ask questions. However, unless the officer has a legal reason, he or she has no right to detain you. This means that if an officer walks up to you, stands in front of you, and begins to ask you questions without suggesting a legal reason for doing so, you can walk away without answering **any** of the questions.

What kinds of circumstances will be considered suspicious by police and what kinds of persons will be considered suspicious-looking? Unfortunately, this depends entirely on the personality and perceptual processes of the particular officer involved. Some people officers may consider it suspicious for any young person to be out at 3:00 in the morning. Other police officers will not consider this to be suspicious unless the person is walking down an alleyway behind business premises where there would be an opportunity for breaking and entering. Again, other officers will consider it suspicious for a person to be seen walking in a skid road area in which drugs are commonly used or for persons who are under age to lurk about a liquor store or licensed premises. Extraordinarily dishevelled appearance, tattooes, motorcycles, or anything of that sort may strike the police officer as suspicious. The number of potentially suspicious circumstances is absolutely infinite and each situation depends entirely on the particular officer involved.

The only generalization that can be made is that a suspicious circumstance can be any situation in which an officer may regard your appearance or behavior as irregular.

1

A good knowledge of your civil rights will help you to handle the situation should you be stopped by the police.

As a general rule, if an officer stops you for no apparent reason and begins to ask questions, you don't have to answer. The law doesn't require you to identify yourself or supply any other information unless the officer can suggest a legal reason for making such a demand. If such a reason is given, it may only go as far as being a legal reason for stopping you and not for asking you questions. Exceptions to this, in most circumstances, are detailed below.

Reasons Given for Stopping People

Canada no longer has the type of vagrancy laws which allow an officer to wantonly stop people and ask them questions about their whereabouts, their economic situations, and places of residence. This does not mean, however, that persons will not be stopped without reason. The commonly used guises for stopping persons who are doing absolutely nothing wrong and about whom there is nothing apparently suspicious is to do it under cover of drug or weapons laws. These laws are sufficiently vague so as to allow police officers to stop people and search on a **reasonable** suspicion that the suspects **might** have drugs or weapons. The reasonableness of an officer's grounds for stopping a person and questioning or searching under the drug or weapons laws is a difficult thing to determine. The statutes themselves do not set out any criteria for determining these things. Clearly the fact that you have a look on your face that the officer does not like is not a reason for allowing him or her to search you for marihuana or weapons. However, police will and do justify unwarranted searches on such grounds as they saw a furtive movement, or some silver paper moving from one person's hand to another person's hand, or something protruding from a pocket which looked like it may have been the butt of a knife.

You cannot be searched unless the police officer has a lawful reason for making a search or you are arrested. If you are not arrested, the officer must state some other lawful reason, such as a belief that you are carrying drugs, liquor, or weapons illegally. You may resist an illegal search, using only as much force as is reasonably necessary. Alternatively, you may inform the officer that you believe the search is illegal and that you do not consent to it. If he or she persists, you may sue in civil law for damages for assault, false arrest, or detention, or charge the officer in criminal law with common assault. Even the threat of this possibility can act as a real deterrent to a rambunctious police officer.

You cannot be held for investigation. Police officers have used this as a guise to arrest persons whom they do not immediately have enough evidence to charge. The police have no right to detain you unless they place you under arrest. If you are under arrest you are charged, not held for investigation. If the police say they wish you to go with them for further investigation, you may go with them. It is up to you, but you are not obliged to go. Obviously, if the officer believes there is evidence to support his or her suspicions, you will be arrested immediately and charged. Then you have no choice. It is in cases where the evidence doesn't justify an arrest on the spot that you may be requested to go to the police station for further investigation. This is not an arrest and you need not obey this request.

It is always a good policy to try to be polite to police officers, even when they don't reciprocate your politeness and proceed without legal justification. If an officer hasn't arrested you and if you don't wish to talk, you can say, "Constable, I don't wish to answer any further questions," and then simply walk away.

One further point -- police officers are obliged to carry their badges with them at all times and it is by this badge number that a particular officer can be identified. If you are stopped, you have the right to demand to see the badge to satisfy yourself that your inquisitor is, in fact, a police officer. You may also ask for that police officer's name. If he or she produces a badge and gives you his or her name, then you should comply with the legal demands.

If the demands are not legal you should inform the officers that you have written down the badge number and his or her name and that you will be contacting the police commission to register a complaint if he or she does not provide a legal reason for stopping you.

It is difficult to enumerate all the various guises under which a police officer may stop you. As mentioned, the usual ones are under the drug laws, weapons laws, or liquor laws which are simple for the police to justify. Formerly, the vagrancy law allowed police to stop and question any suspicious-looking persons. Vagrancy was a summary offence under the Criminal Code and included the charge of wandering or trespassing with no apparent means of support and failing to justify your presence to a police officer when required to do so. It enabled an officer to stop you any place and demand that you justify your presence. You did not have the right to remain silent because failure to explain your presence would be held against you. This was formerly one of the commonest means for stopping persons without cause. Now that it is gone, greater use will certainly be made of the drug laws, weapons laws, and liquor laws.

In municipalities where a curfew is in effect for young people, a perfect guise is provided for police officers to stop, question, and search young persons.

Extraordinary situations, such as when we had the War Measures Act invoked, provide police with all the grounds they need to stop and question any person at any time and the threat to one's civil liberties is extreme. However, it is an extraordinary situation and hopefully will be used very sparingly and only when the national security is in jeopardy.

Police officers may also stop persons and charge them with causing a disturbance, for example, impeding or obstructing pedestrian or vehicular traffic. Presumably, if you are standing on a sidewalk in such a manner that persons must walk around you to continue in their path, you may be causing a disturbance. A police officer who wishes to search you could conceivably use such a reason to stop you and ask you questions. You do not have to answer these questions unless the officer states that you are under arrest.

Occasionally young people are stopped by police because of municipal hitch-hiking laws. Some hitch-hiking practices are illegal. It is, for example, illegal to stand in the roadway for the purpose of soliciting a ride. Standing on the edge of a sidewalk or on the shoulder of the road if there is no sidewalk is okay. Hitch-hiking on a freeway is always illegal.

Unless you are suspected of another offence, you will probably get a warning the first time you are stopped for illegal hitch-hiking. Police officers have been known to circle the block after giving such a warning. If you are still standing in the roadway when they come by again, you will probably get a ticket. They don't have to arrest you but if they do, they have a right to search you. You don't have to answer any questions.

Provincial motor-vehicle laws authorize police to stop any motor-vehicle and ask the driver to produce his or her driver's licence, vehicle registration, and insurance evidence. If you drive a vehicle, always be prepared to produce these three documents. You may also be asked the name and address of the driver and owner of the vehicle. The police have no right to question passengers unless one of the passengers happens to also be the owner. Then the police can only ask the questions listed above.

If the police try to search the car, ask to see a search warrant. If they inform you they are searching under the drug, weapons, or liquor laws, they may have the right to proceed without a warrant if they have grounds. Otherwise, they have no right to search a vehicle without a warrant and you may resist the search, using such force as is reasonably necessary in the circumstances to resist the search successfully.

House Searches

A search by police officers for soft drugs is the commonest reason given for invading a person's privacy in an apartment or home. This can be done without a search warrant or a writ of assistance. (Both of these documents are dealt with in chapter VII which discusses the drug laws in detail.) It is under the drug laws that most of the searches of houses or other residences are made although a search may also be made for stolen property. In this case, the police must have a warrant.

CHAPTER II

THE LAW OF ARREST

Most drug charges, including possession of marihuana and hashish, heroin, cocaine, LSD, MDA, and so on can be tried summarily or by indictment, at the option of the prosecutor. Therefore, you should always treat these as indictable offences which are the most serious and carry heavier penalties than summary offences. An **indictable offence** in Canada is similar to a felony in the United States; a **summary offence** in Canada is more like a misdemeanor in the United States (see chapter XV for further explanation of indictable and summary offences).

Shoplifting and other theft charges, charges of breaking and entering, obtaining by false pretences, forgery, obstructing or assaulting a police officer, escaping custody, perjury, treason, sedition, and so on are indictable. Most weapons charges can be either summary or indictable although some are only indictable. Most sexual offences, such as statutory rape, are indictable. Summary offences include causing a disturbance, unlawful assembly, hitchhiking and all motor vehicle offences under provincial laws, nudity in a public place, liquor charges under provincial law, common assault, and soliciting for the purpose of prostitution. You can be arrested for a summary offence if you are found committing it, or on the basis of a warrant which has been issued for your arrest.

In order to make a lawful arrest, the arresting officer should identify himself or herself, state that you are being arrested, and touch you to indicate that you are in custody. You must be informed of the reason for the arrest or be shown the warrant, where feasible. (For example, it isn't feasible if you are running from a bank with a gun in one hand, and a mask and pillowcase in the other. In this case the reason for the arrest is obvious.)

In Canada, it is completely legal to refuse to comply with the attempts of a police officer to effect an illegal arrest.

If the officer grabs you by the shoulder and refuses to state a legal reason for the arrest, you may resist. You may use as much force as is reasonably necessary to escape his or her grasp. (In some states in the United States there are what are called "no-sock" laws. These laws make it an offence to resist an illegal arrest, and you can be guilty of violating a no-sock law even if you merely go limp and resist passively.)

However, resisting an illegal arrest can be hazardous. It may result in a charge of assaulting or obstructing a police officer. If the arrest is illegal, you have a defence to these charges; but if you don't have witnesses, there is a danger that your testimony may not be believed in court and you may be convicted.

It is very important in situations in which a friend of yours is being arrested and you are standing by, that you do not interfere unduly with the police officer. And it is very good practice to remain present at a situation like that to make sure that the police officer does not abuse the rights of your friend. If you are certain that the police officer is doing an illegal act toward your friend, such as assaulting him or her without provocation or justification, then you can interfere to assist your friend in resisting such an assault. But if a police officer is merely talking to your friend, asking questions, or placing him or her under arrest, you cannot interfere in any way or you may be charged with obstructing a police officer. If you are so charged, you can be convicted as long as the police officer can show that he or she was obstructed by your actions.

Citizens' Arrest

Any citizen, including a store detective or a private security officer, has a limited power of arrest. He or she may arrest a person found committing an indictable offence, or a person believed, on reasonable and probable grounds, to be committing a criminal offence and being chased by police.

A citizen who makes an arrest is under obligation to deliver the arrested person forthwith to a police officer. This means that he or she must turn the arrested person over to police as soon as possible. Failure to do this makes the arrest illegal and the arrested person may sue for damages.

By far the most common form of citizens' arrest occurs in cases of shoplifting. Store detectives can arrest you if they find you committing the act of shoplifting. They have, however, no right to search you and must turn you over to the police forthwith.

If you are innocent of shoplifting you may choose to resist the arrest by a store detective, using such force as is necessary to obtain your freedom. Sometimes it may be wiser to follow another course. If you object verbally to the arrest and are later released, or acquitted of the charge, you can bring civil suit against the particular store detective, and against the store itself, for damages for assault, defamation of character, false imprisonment, and malicious prosecution.

CHAPTER III

SEARCH AND SEIZURE IN THE CRIMINAL CODE

The general rule in the Criminal Code is that police have no right to search a place without a warrant. There are, however, exceptions to this rule under federal weapons, customs, and drug laws, and under provincial liquor laws. These exceptions are dealt with in further detail in later chapters.

Search warrants are issued only by justices of the peace, provincial court judges, or magistrates. To obtain a search warrant, an officer must swear a document informing the judge that he or she suspects a particular offence has been committed and believes evidence can be found in a certain house, building, car, or other place. The evidence must be specified. The warrant must state the officer's name, the anticipated charge, the premises to be searched, the owner or occupier of the premises, and the evidence to be searched for. The warrant will bear the date that it is issued by the justice of the peace.

If police arrive at your door with a search warrant, you should ask to see the warrant. They are obliged to carry it with them, to produce it and allow you to examine it upon request. Often they will have a duplicate copy of the warrant which they will give to you if you request it. If you let them in without asking to see the warrant, it is absolutely useless to object later that they did not show you the warrant or give you a copy of it. The time to object is when they arrive.

You should check carefully to see that the warrant does, indeed, set out an offence and that your name and place of residence are correctly stated. If the address on the warrant is not your address, the police have no right to enter and you should tell them so. If the warrant shows your address, but names someone else as occupant, you can refuse entry.

Check the date -- warrants are valid on the day specified and for a reasonable time thereafter. If the search is being made more than two days after the date on which the warrant was obtained, you should seek legal counsel as it may be that the validity of the search warrant can be challenged on this basis. Make sure that the officer to whom the warrant is directed is present. A warrant must be executed by day -- between sunrise and sunset -- unless it specifically provides for execution by night.

Search warrants under the Criminal Code permit an officer to search a place, house, apartment, or car. They do not allow an officer to search a person. If an officer tries to search you, you may ask if you are under arrest. If you are told that you are not, you may refuse to be searched. There is no general power to search an individual who is not under arrest.

When police complete the search, which you must permit them to do if the warrant is correctly issued, they must take anything they have seized before the person who issued the warrant. They must also file a written report stating what was found and what happened during the search.

If your house is searched often, and no charges are laid, you can complain to the police commission, or sue the officers in civil court for damages for trespass.

In general, to search a motor-vehicle, police are in exactly the same position as they are in searching houses and apartments. That is, they must go before a justice of the peace, provincial court judge, or magistrate and swear an information document specifying the motor-vehicle to be searched. However, arbitrary searches of motor-vehicles can be justifiably carried out under the drug, liquor, customs, and weapons laws.

CHAPTER IV

THE CONSEQUENCES OF AN ARREST

Once you have been legally arrested, your situation changes markedly. The police have the power to search you, and will usually do so. They will frisk you on the street and then take you to the station where you may be booked, stripped, and skin-frisked.

On arrest, police officers should warn you that you will be charged with ''x'' offence, and that you needn't say anything, but that anything you do say may be given in evidence against you. This warning is not a legal requirement in

Canada, but if you are not warned, and you make incriminating statements, a judge may use this as a reason to find your statements inadmissible as evidence against you. It depends on the total circumstances of the arrest and interrogation whether the judge throws out an admission because of the "lack of warning" or allows it in as evidence. Also, some police officers may not warn you because they feel that an accused person who is warned will be reluctant to make statements. A police officer making an arrest may, therefore, avoid giving you the warning until he or she has asked you a number of questions, the answers to which may be self-incriminating.

Whether or not you are warned, the best advice is to remain silent. You may tell an officer who questions you that you have nothing to say until you consult a lawyer.

There may be instances in which you do not wish to remain silent. You may be innocent of the charge, or you may know that the police have arrested the wrong man. In these circumstances, you may well deem it wise to tell them so immediately and offer an explanation or alibi concerning the offence for which you are being arrested. Certainly a judge is more inclined to accept your alibi if it was offered at the first opportunity, but you should be sure of your facts before you state where you were at the time of the alleged offence.

It is also advantageous to make a statement if you are arrested for possession of stolen property. The arresting officer will demand that you explain how you came to be in possession of the property. If you didn't know the goods were stolen, tell the officer. The fact that you gave an explanation at the time of arrest will weigh in your favor in court. If you received the goods in circumstances that now strike you as suspicious, you may wish to tell the officer you will happily make a statement after consulting a lawyer.

One curious bit of law in Canada refers to the charge of possession of instruments suitable for the purpose of housebreaking, vault-breaking, or safe-breaking. The way the law reads, anyone who is in possession of such an instrument, for example, a screwdriver, under circumstances that cause a police officer to make a reasonable inference that the instrument has been used or is or was intended to be used for housebreaking, vault-breaking, or safe-breaking can be arrested and charged with the offence and will be presumed to be guilty of that offence unless he or she can establish a lawful excuse for being in possession of the instrument under the circumstances. There are very few cases under this section and nothing to indicate what will be considered to be circumstances giving rise to a reasonable inference that the instrument was used or is being used or was intended to be used for the purpose of housebreaking. If you are observed by a police officer late at night with a screwdriver in your back pocket or any similar tool in your possession and you are in the vicinity of an area in which there may be housebreaking or some other breaking, you can be arrested for possession of instruments for the purpose of housebreaking. Should this happen, you may wish to explain why you have the screwdriver or other implement in your possession. If your explanation satisfies the officer, you may not be charged. However, if you are not charged, you should remember what you have read earlier in this chapter.

Finally, if you are a juvenile, you should tell the police your age (see chapter XX which deals fully with the criminal law position of juveniles). In juvenile court, bail is easier, penalties are more lenient, and you don't receive a criminal record. If you let the court believe that you are an adult, your conviction may stand even if you are below the age at which you can be charged in adult court.

There are other circumstances in which you may wish to make a statement. In any case, if you are innocent and are sufficiently knowledgeable of the law to know that you are legally innocent, you may wish to inform the officer of this situation. Most persons are not too adept at dealing with the law authorities and do not know their way around the law that well, so they are advised by lawyers not to make statements. Persons who are well informed of the law have very little to fear for they know where they tread when they speak. Unless you feel sufficiently certain of your position, it is always better to consult a lawyer before saying anything.

CHAPTER V

THE NARCOTICS LAWS

Illegal possession and distribution of drugs are two of the crimes most commonly committed in North America. While the use of drugs threatens to become as widespread as the use of alcohol, it still remains illegal. The drug laws, like earlier prohibition laws, are virtually impossible to enforce. The number of people "busted" under the existing drug laws is minimal in comparison with the countless numbers who choose to defy the law and use illegal drugs.

It is not the purpose of this book to condone or condemn the use of illegal drugs. Our purpose is to tell you what these drugs are and where you stand, legally, in connection with them.

The Narcotic Control Act bans the use of cannabis marihuana, cannabis resin (hashish), cannabinol, pyrohexyl, and tetrahydrocannabinol (THC). It also bans opium, codeine, morphine, diacetylmorphine (heroin), and cocaine.

Marihuana consists of the flowering tops, leaves, seeds and stems of the hemp plant. It grows easily throughout North America and in most other countries of the world.

Hashish is the pure resin of the marihuana plant and is available in solid or liquid form. THC, or tetrahydro-cannabinol, is the active ingredient of marihuana. It can be synthesized and comes in capsule, powder, or liquid form. There is very little pure THC available.

Opium is derived from the dried juices of the seeds of the opium poppy. Morphine and codeine are derivatives of opium and heroin is a derivative of morphine. Cocaine is a derivative of the South American coca plant.

Possession of any of these drugs, for other than medicinal purposes, is an offence under the Narcotic Control Act and you may be proceeded against either summarily or by indictment at the election of the prosecutor. If you are brought before the court, the prosecutor will choose to proceed by summary offence where, for example, a small amount of narcotics is involved and it is your first offence. The maximum penalties for a summary offence are a fine of $1,000, imprisonment for one year, or both.

In most parts of Canada, if you are convicted of possession of a small amount of marihuana and it is your first offence, you will probably receive a fine, or probation, or both. If you are convicted of a second offence, the penalty will be stiffer, and could be a gaol term.

Trafficking in a narcotic is an indictable offence and carries a maximum penalty of life imprisonment. The definition of trafficking is very wide. It includes manufacturing, selling, giving, administering, transporting, sending, delivering, or distributing. It also includes offering to do any of these things, e.g., offering to give someone a joint.

If you are arrested and charged with trafficking, it is very probable that you will be alleged to have sold the drugs to an undercover agent. In these circumstances, you should say nothing other than to demand the right to telephone your lawyer. Trafficking, even in so-called "soft drugs," is treated very seriously by the courts. To illustrate, a man on the West Coast recently received the maximum sentence of life imprisonment for his **first** offence of trafficking. Judges are imposing stiffer sentences in this regard and a word to the wise should be sufficient.

The law does not state what amount of narcotics will take you from a charge of mere possession to a charge of possession with intent to traffic. Usually, you will not be charged with possession with intent unless you have several ounces of grass or a smaller amount divided into small individual packages. It will depend upon the circumstances. The law, as it is presently constituted, is stacked against you when you are charged with possession for the purpose of trafficking. Once the court finds that you were in possession of a sufficiently large amount, you are presumed guilty of possession with intent to traffic unless you can prove otherwise. In these circumstances, you can call evidence to suggest that you are a heavy user of the particular drug or that you have plenty of money and do not need to traffic to earn more, and so on.

One further comment should be made. In cases of trafficking or possession with intent to traffic, it is not necessarily a defence that the drug, when analyzed, proves not to be the drug you claimed to be selling. For example, suppose you have a drug which you believe is cocaine. You sell it to someone, perhaps an undercover police officer, and it is analyzed as heroin, another narcotic. The prosecutor can charge you with trafficking in a drug which **you held out to be cocaine** and the court can convict you.

The cultivation of marihuana plants is also an offence. It is indictable and carries a maximum penalty of seven year. The Narcotic Control Act gives the Minister of National Health and Welfare the power to order destruction of any growing plant of opium poppy or marihuana that has not been cultivated under lawfully issued licence.

It should be noted also that **importing** is the heaviest charge under the Narcotic Control Act. A conviction for importing a narcotic into Canada, or exporting a narcotic out of Canada, carries **a minimum** penalty of seven years in gaol. The **maximum** sentence is life imprisonment.

CHAPTER VI

THE FOOD AND DRUG ACT

All the hallucinogen drugs, with the exception of tobacco and alcohol, are restricted under schedule H of the Food and Drug Act. They include LSD, MDA, DMT, DET, MMDA, and LBJ. New drugs of similar nature are added to the list from time to time, the most recent additions being DET, MMDA, and LBJ. None of these drugs may be legally in your possession unless they are prescribed by a qualified physician.

Should you be charged with illegal possession of any restricted drug such as LSD or MDA, the prosecutor may proceed against you by either summary or indictable offence rules, just as for possession of narcotics. If the prosecutor chooses to proceed against you summarily, the maximum penalties for a first offence are a fine of $1,000, or imprisonment for six months, or both. For a subsequent offence the penalties are, again, the same as possession of marihuana -- a maximum fine of $2,000, or imprisonment for twelve months, or both. If you are charged with an indictable offence, the maximum penalties are a fine of $5,000, or imprisonment for three years, or both. The penalties are lighter than for an indictable offence of possession under the Narcotic Control Act. However, most judges will impose much the same sentence for possession of LSD as for possession of marihuana.

Amphetamines, methamphetamines, benzamphetamines and the barbiturates generally -- the "uppers" and "downers" -- are controlled drugs under schedule G of the Food and Drug Act. The most common amphetamines are dexadrine, benzedrine, methedrine, and dexamyl.

The barbiturates are depressants, commonly known as "downers." They are used medically as sleeping pills and tranquilizers.

It is not an offence to be in possession of amphetamine, benzamphetamine, methamphetamine, or the barbiturates. The only offences in connection with these drugs are trafficking or possession with intent to traffic.

If you are charged with trafficking or possession with intent to traffic a controlled or restricted drug, the prosecutor has the option of proceeding against you summarily or by indictment. If he or she proceeds summarily, the maximum penalty is three years. However, the prosecutor, in these circumstances, usually proceeds by indictment.

Under the Food and Drug Act, the term "to traffic" means to manufacture, sell, export, import, transport, or deliver. In this case the definition does not specifically include giving. Also in this case, importing is not a separate offence from trafficking and, therefore, **does not** carry the heavy seven-year minimum penalty provided in the Narcotic Control Act.

It is, of course, illegal to traffic in a drug held out to be a restricted or prohibited drug.

Some drugs are legal in Canada. At the time of writing, the hallucinogens known as psilocybin, amanita muscaria and peyote are all legal. Psilocybin is extracted from a mushroom fungus and is available in liquid or powder form. Amanita muscaria is the so-called "magic mushroom." Peyote comes from button-shaped growths on a certain cactus plant that grows in Mexico and southwest United States. It is used in religious ceremonies of the Native American Church. Peyote and psilocybin are banned by federal drug laws in the United States. None of the drugs mentioned above are readily available in Canada.

Mescaline, a natural alkaloid found in the same cactus plant as peyote, is legal to **possess** in Canada. It is available in dry powder form and can also be made chemically. However, the danger of chemically-produced mescaline is that most of what is sold in Canada analyzes to an impure form of LSD. The **sale** of mescaline is illegal.

Morning Glory seeds, which contain a small amount of psychotropic substance, are also legal in Canada. Because it is necessary to consume a tremendous quantity of Morning Glory seeds to obtain any effect, the government feels there is no threat of widespread usage.

CHAPTER VII

THE DRUG LAWS -- SEARCH AND SEIZURE

Under the Narcotic Control Act, the police have wide powers to search for illegal drugs. They can search, without a warrant, any place that is not a residence. They can also search any person found in such place. To do these things, however, the police officers must first have a reasonable belief that they will find illegal drugs. The law provides no criteria for determining what a "reasonable belief" may be.

The law, as it stands, is capable of a number of bizarre possibilities. What is a "place"? Does the law mean police can search anyone, anywhere, any time? The word "place" is open to wide interpretation. It isn't restricted to a car, or any other vehicle, or any building that is not a residence. It could mean any place, for example a public plaza, a shopping centre, a street, a park, a department store, or a parking lot.

How do you deal with a drug search when the police officers have no warrant? The usual rules apply. The police officer must inform you of his or her lawful reason for detaining you. If he or she can't suggest one, you can walk away. If you are told "drugs," you should ask, "What drugs?" If you are told "narcotics," you should ask, "What narcotics?" But if the officer insists, you have no option. You must permit the search. At this point you should not answer any questions until you talk to a lawyer. Possession is a technical matter in law and an offhand statement may get you into trouble in court.

If your car is stopped by a police officer who asks you to get out so he or she can search, you may object and ask to see a search warrant. If the officer does not have one but is planning to search under either the Narcotic Control Act, or the Food and Drug Act, then you can ask on what grounds. Then, if the officer persists, let him or her go ahead. You do not have to answer questions about who owns anything which may be in the vehicle.

The Narcotic Control Act authorizes police to seize a conveyance, such as a motor car, in which a narcotic is found. When this happens, and a person is convicted of an offence of trafficking, possession for the purpose of trafficking, importing, or exporting a narcotic, the court can order that the vehicle used for the offence be forfeited to the state. The owner of the vehicle, however, can appeal against this order.

If the police are not making a search under the Narcotic Control Act or under another law which must be stated, then the search is illegal and your right to due process is being abused.

You may, in these circumstances, defend your property using only as much force as is reasonably necessary to prevent the illegal search. Unless you have something to gain by resisting, it is probably better to go along and take legal remedies later. It should be borne in mind that evidence obtained from an illegal search is, nevertheless, admissible in Canadian courts and, therefore, the time to object to an illegal search is when the police propose to inflict it upon you.

Police officers have no right to search your residence for illegal drugs unless they have a search warrant or a writ of assistance. A mobile home or a tent is your residence if you happen to live there. The police must have a reasonable belief that there is an illegal drug in your premises before searching.

A writ of assistance is issued by the federal court to a named officer of the Royal Canadian Mounted Police. It alows the officer to search any residence at any time for narcotics or controlled or restricted drugs -- and that writ is valid until the officer leaves the force. No other officer may use the writ, although the named officer may take others to assist in a raid. However, in such a raid, the named officer must have the writ with him or her.

At the time of writing this book there are 210 writs of assistance issued under the drug laws to officers of the RCMP. There are 53 in Ontario, 52 in British Columbia, and 35 in Quebec. Alberta has 15 and Saskatchewan, the Maritimes, and the Territories each have less than 15. These writs of assistance are also authorized under the federal income tax and customs laws.

If police knock at your door and request entry, ask first if they have a search warrant (see chapter III). If they say they have a writ of assistance, ask to see it, and ask the officer named therein to identify himself or herself.

While a search is proceeding, you may wish to make notes on the activities of the officers involved. You may need them to refresh your memory if you are later in court. Both the Narcotic Control Act and the Food and Drug Act authorize police to break doors, windows, locks, fasteners, floors, walls, ceilings, compartments, plumbing fixtures, boxes, containers, or anything else they consider to be relevant to their search. If they break doors unnecessarily, you may sue for recovery of the damage.

CHAPTER VIII

DRUG TRIALS --
WHAT THE PROSECUTOR MUST PROVE

When you are charged with possession of marihuana, the first chore of the prosecutor is to prove the drug itself. A chemist must be engaged to prove that the substance you had was, in fact, marihuana.

A certificate of analysis may be served on you a reasonable time before trial, usually a week. This certificate will enable the prosecutor to prove the drug without calling in the analyst to give evidence.

As long as there is enough dope to analyze, no matter how small the amount, you may be convicted. Police constantly bust known addicts and seize spoons or hypodermic kits containing a miniscule amount of heroin. Soft drug searches are often fruitless except for pipes with a residue of grass or hash. This residue is sufficient for analysis. A few seeds or stems will support a charge of possession.

If you haven't confessed to the offence, the prosecutor is obliged to prove all of the following points:

(a)   that you knew the particular drug was marihuana or whatever

(b)   that you knew the location, either on your person or elsewhere, of the particular drug

(c)   that your possession was voluntary

(d)   that you had some measure of control over the drug and its whereabouts

These are the essential elements of legal possession. If proof of any one of them is lacking, you will be acquitted.

For example, suppose you are searched under the Narcotic Control Act and the officer finds a capsule of white powder in your pocket. You say that the cap is LSD but it is analyzed as heroin, and you are charged with possession of heroin. In the absence of other incriminating evidence, such as needle or "track" marks on your arm, you will probably be acquitted. The real problem in a case like this is that you may be forced to give evidence, in which case the judge may disbelieve you and convict you.

In one case, narcotics officers entered a room occupied by two men. The accused was in bed, and his room-mate wasn't home. During the search, the officers found a bag of grass in the third drawer of a four-drawer dresser. When they asked the accused if he knew what it was he admitted that it looked like marihuana. Then they asked him if he had exclusive use of any drawers in the dresser and he said that he used the two bottom draws. They asked if the bag of grass was his and he said, "If you found it in the bottom two drawers, it must be mine."

At the trial, the officers gave the accused's statements and further testified as follows:

"We searched two drawers and found nothing. In the third drawer we found a bag of green plant-like material (which was analyzed as marihuana)."

The judge acquitted the accused because no proof was offered that the bag was found in the **bottom** two drawers -- the "third drawer" could have been the third from either top or bottom of the dresser. Even though the accused admitted that he owned whatever was found in the bottom two drawers, there was no evidence that he had knowledge of or control over anything in the drawer second from the top, which could be third from the bottom.

The issue of voluntariness may also arise in this way. Suppose somebody mails you a pound of hash you did not know about, or want. The narcotics officers burst in two minutes after the mailman has left. You are holding the wrapper with your name and address on it and the opened package of dope is sitting on the table because you haven't yet decided how to get rid of it. The prosecutor will have trouble establishing that you were expecting the package or that you intended to keep it. You would testify that you were an involuntary possessor. For an acquittal, the judge must believe your evidence, or at least harbor doubt as to your guilt.

Where both elements of knowledge are proved and there is some evidence of voluntariness, there may be a defence based upon control. Suppose that you are visiting friends, and there is some marihuana on the kitchen table. You are the only person sitting at the table when narcotics officers arrive but you are a visitor and have no right to the dope and no control over its use.

In this case the owner of the dope may take the protection against self-incrimination offered by the Canada Evidence Act and give evidence at your trial.

Section 5 of the Canada Evidence Act allows him or her to refuse to answer incriminating questions until the judge grants protection. A person testifying under the Canada Evidence Act must ask for the protection of that act for each question which may require an incriminating answer. In these circumstances, you won't be convicted. You are not in possession unless the prosecutor proves that you had a measure of control over the drug.

CHAPTER IX

SEARCH AND SEIZURE
UNDER THE LIQUOR LAWS

Liquor laws vary somewhat from province to province. Offences under these laws are summary and usually result in a fine for the first or second conviction. They include consuming liquor or being drunk in a public place, possession in an unlicensed dining room or club, possession of unsealed liquor, illegal sale or bootlegging, sale or supplying of liquor to a minor, being a minor in a liquor store or beer parlour, being a minor purchasing, possessing, or consuming liquor.

Police acting under provincial liquor laws may search automobiles without a warrant. They need only have a suspicion that the automobile contains illegal liquor or that liquor is kept in the automobile for an unlawful purpose. In most provinces they can also search a person's land, except for dwelling houses, without a warrant. These laws also permit search of persons found in a car, or on land, where liquor violations are suspected.

Under the liquor laws, police officers need a warrant to search a dwelling. To obtain the warrant they must have reasonable grounds for believing that a liquor violation is occurring in the dwelling, but they need not give reasons for their suspicion or belief. A warrant enables officers to enter any part of the building.

There are variations in the laws in various provinces. In Manitoba, for example, police searching a building or premises may require found-ins to give their names and addresses. In Ontario, police may search persons in a place they have entered with a warrant. In British Columbia, you may not be searched until you have been arrested.

The rules for objecting to searches under provincial liquor laws are the same as for other searches. Police must state a reason for the search. You should demand to see the warrant. Check it to see that it specifies your house and yourself, and that it bears the proper dates. If it is accurate, let the police in. You may make note of their activities and you may refuse to answer questions until you talk to a lawyer.

Supplying liquor to a minor is a serious matter. You may be charged under the Juvenile Delinquents Act with the summary offence of contributing to juvenile delinquency. This carries a maximum penalty of two years' imprisonment. The only time a minor can legally drink is when the liquor is supplied by a parent or guardian at home.

CHAPTER X

SEARCH AND SEIZURE
UNDER THE CUSTOMS LAWS

Many people coming into Canada, either Canadians returning to Canada or visitors to this country, are stopped at the border, questioned, and searched. Persons entering Canada must do so legally and can bring with them only what the law entitles them to bring. They can be questioned as to what their legal right to enter is, that is, whether they are Canadian citizens, landed immigrants, holders of visitors' visas, or on a short holiday from the United States. Immigration officials can inspect their passports or other identification documents to confirm their right to enter.

The Canadian Customs Act gives officers very wide powers to investigate smuggling. Acting upon information or upon reasonable grounds of suspicion, which is not defined by the Customs Act, an officer may hold, open, and examine any package suspected of containing prohibited property or smuggled goods. The officer may board any sea vessel or enter any vehicle entering Canada, or within Canada, and search for prohibited or smuggled goods. He or she has power to seize a vessel or vehicle attachments containing contraband goods.

Customs officers may also search any building, yard, or other place after swearing before a justice of the peace that they have reasonable cause to suspect that goods liable to seizure and forfeiture are in such place. The Customs Act provides that they must first ask for permission to enter and then, if this is denied, they may forcibly enter. They may seize all prohibited and smuggled goods.

With a writ of assistance, a customs officer may enter any time of the day or night any building or other place to search for and seize goods that he or she has reasonable grounds to believe are liable to forfeiture under the act. To effect a search, the officer may break open any doors, chests, or packages that he or she deems necessary.

A customs officer may arrest without warrant anyone found committing, or suspected of having committed, any indictable offence under the Customs Act or the Criminal Code.

There are very wide powers for a search of a person. A customs officer may search anyone on board a vessel within a port of Canada, or in a vehicle entering Canada by land, or anyone who has come into Canada from a foreign country in any way whatever, if the officer has reasonable cause to suppose that the person has goods which must be disclosed at customs, or prohibited goods, on his or her person. The law provides that a person who is going to be searched by a customs officer may demand that the officer take him or her before a police magistrate, justice of the peace, or chief customs officer. One of these authorities must then decide if there is reasonable cause for the search and, if there is not, discharge the person. The act provides that a female shall be searched by a female officer.

The Customs Act also protects customs officers from being sued in civil courts and sets out a specific manner in which these persons can be sued. If the judge finds, in a civil suit, that the defendant customs officer acted on probable cause, the plaintiff is not entitled to more than twenty cents damages.

CHAPTER XI

BAIL

The word "bail" has traditionally been used for the situation in which a person is released from custody pending trial. The word itself may be going out of use as the Criminal Code now refers to the act of obtaining bail from a court as "judicial interim release" rather than "bail."

The Bill of Rights guarantees your right to have a reasonable bail. This right cannot be denied without just cause. The Bill of Rights does not resolve the question of what is reasonable bail nor does it settle the question of what is just cause for denying bail. The amendments to the bail provisions of the Criminal Code which were made early in 1972 render it a cinch that bail will be granted in every case unless there is a very good reason against granting it. Where formerly the accused had to justify to the court that he or she should be released on bail by showing that the offence was not very serious, that he or she had no previous criminal record, lived in the community, and would be certain to turn up for trial, now it is the prosecutor who must satisfy the court that the accused will not turn up for trial or will commit another offence if permitted out on bail. The prosecutor must prove that the accused should be kept in custody or else the accused will be released by the court. There are still a lot of problems in enforcing the new bail bill as a lot of the judges and prosecutors, and even defence counsels, do not understand it. Many of the accused who have been arrested in previous years are very surprised to find that they are released with such ease under the new bail law. Parliament has finally gotten around to giving some consideration to what it said in the Bill of Rights. The new bail provisions in the Criminal Code go a long way toward realizing the guarantee of bail in the Bill of Rights.

The important considerations are still and will always be the seriousness of the charge and the likelihood that you

41

will turn up for your trial. When you are charged with an offence for which you will receive a term of imprisonment, such as armed robbery or manslaughter, higher bail will be set. You can be released on bail even on charges of murder. However, if it appears that a substantial term of imprisonment is likely, then you will probably be denied bail. If it is suspected that you will jump bail, you will be kept in custody. Apart from the severity of the charge, the court's concern will be whether or not you have roots in the community which will tend to show that you will turn up for your trial. You are in a better position if you have a job, a residence, a family, relatives, or property in the community -- things to tie you to the area. Your record will also be considered. If you have a previous record for skipping bail, bail will be set high or may be denied. Where previously a criminal record, if it was bad, would crucify a person who applied for bail, in the present situation, unless the record is for such offences as skipping bail or escaping custody, it may help as much as hinder. There are some persons around who have such lengthy criminal records that they have been to court as many times as court reporters and possibly have come on time to court more than the court reporters have. There is no justification for denying these persons bail simply because of their criminal record, unless the prosecutor can show some cogent grounds for suspecting the person will commit another criminal offence while out on bail.

In any situation where you are charged with a summary offence, have no criminal record, and have lived in the area for a little while or have a job, you will probably not even be arrested. Police officers are directed by the Criminal Code not to arrest persons charged with summary offences, offences which may be summary or indictable, or indictable offences which must be tried by a magistrate (such as theft under $200 and assaulting or obstructing a police officer) unless they can show that the arrest is necessary to establish the accused's identity, secure or preserve evidence relating to the charge, prevent the continuation of the offence, or prevent the commission of another offence.

Police officers must also be satisfied that the person, if not arrested, will fail to attend in court. This means that in such circumstances as those cited here, police officers will more than likely release the person by the issuance of an appearance notice.

It is when you are a transient person with no fixed address, job, or ties in the community, or when the alleged charge is very serious and conviction will result in a term of imprisonment that you may have to go to court for the setting of bail.

Now, a police officer who arrests a person even for an indictable offence still must release the person by summons or appearance notice unless the officer can establish one of the following grounds: that there is a need to identify the person, preserve evidence, or prevent the continuation or commission of another offence or that he or she believes that the person will not attend at court if released. In these cases only will a suspect be detained.

An officer-in-charge of a police force also has the power to release persons outright with the intention of issuing a summons, or have the person sign a promise to appear, or release the person on a recognizance without sureties* to an amount not exceeding $500 but without deposit of money. (This means that the person charged merely signs a form agreeing to return to court when required. If the accused fails to appear when required, the state has a legal right to collect the amount up to $500 from the accused. For example, an accused who is, say, released on a $200 recognizance, is agreeing to pay the court $200 if he or she fails to appear. The other consequence of failing to appear may be more dire -- trial for a summary offence.) If the accused does not live in the province or does not live within 100 miles of the gaol where he or she has been charged, the officer-in-charge can release the accused on a cash recognizance without sureties in an amount not exceeding $500.

*Surety means a person other than the accused, such as a friend or relative of the accused, who signs a recognizance to obtain the release of the accused on bail. Courts generally require sureties where they feel the accused cannot be relied upon to turn up for his or her trial or where there is a danger the accused might commit another offence. Where the court does not require a surety, the accused can be released simply by his or her own signature. If the court does require a surety, the recognizance must be signed by other than the accused. Traditionally, the courts have felt that the surety, who stands to lose money if the accused fails to appear for trial, will guarantee, in some way, the presence or the return of the accused.

In this situation, the officer can demand a deposit of the stated sum. The officer-in-charge can release a person in the same circumstances as the arresting officer as well as a person charged with an indictable offence punishable by imprisonment for five years or less. Such an offence is possession of a weapon for a purpose dangerous to the public peace. An officer-in-charge can justify detention on the same grounds, i.e., that it is necessary to keep the person in custody in the public interest or because the person may fail to attend court for trial. A person who is arrested and not released by the arresting officer or by the officer-in-charge must be brought before a justice of the peace, magistrate, or provincial court judge within twenty-four hours. In relation to any offence where the maximum penalty is seven, ten, or fourteen years or life imprisonment, the matter of bail will always reach this stage. For example, cases of theft over $200, breaking and entering, trafficking in a narcotic, and other cases of this sort all come under this category. The court will hold what is called a "show cause" hearing at which the prosecutor will have to show cause why the detention of the accused in custody is justified. If he or she cannot do so, the accused will be released on a simple undertaking to appear for trial. Where a prosecutor can show reasons why the accused should not be released on a simple undertaking, the accused may be released on an undertaking with conditions, such as reporting to a police officer every week or by having some responsible person in the community sign a "recognizance" for the accused which may or may not be backed by bail money. Cash bail will be set only if the person does not reside within 100 miles of the gaol or in the province. If the prosecutor is successful in showing cause why the detention of the accused in custody is justified, the justice can make that order but must include in the record a statement of his or her reasons for making an order. The order can be appealed. Detention is justified only on the grounds that it is necessary so that the accused will turn up in court for trial or on the ground that it is necessary in the public interest because of a likelihood that the accused might commit another crime or interfere with the administration of justice by, for example, threatening witnesses.

A comment should be made on the situation of a surety bail. A surety is a person who signs a recognizance to guarantee your return to court. If you don't show up, the surety must pay the sum stated in the recognizance to the Crown. Suppose you were released on a $500 bond with one surety and a friend owes the Crown $500. If the justice of the peace doesn't believe your friend has $500 at the time of putting up the bail, he or she may demand proof of it. Proof can be tendered by bank documents indicating an amount of money on deposit in the friend's account or by property deeds which are commonly left with the court clerks as security for high bails.

If you don't get bail, you must appear before a judge or justice every eight days until your trial. If you are granted bail on your own undertaking or recognizance, interim appearances before trial are not required. If you have a surety or a bondsman, interim appearances are required every eight days unless the bondsman consents to a remand directly to the trial date. Where the bail is an undertaking or something to that effect, you can consent yourself to the case going over directly to the trial date.

You must make the required appearances. If you fail to appear at the time when you are required in court, a bench warrant will be issued for your arrest. Bail may be cancelled and you may be remanded into custody to await trial. You may also be charged with failing to attend court or with what is commonly known as skipping bail. A conviction for skipping bail usually carries as penalty a term of imprisonment.

If you fail to appear on a summary offence for trial, the trial can proceed in your absence. You may be convicted in your absence or fined or given a term of imprisonment, in which case a warrant will be issued for your arrest.

If your bail is in cash or property which you can't raise or if a surety is required, you will need friends. Canada does not have professional bondspersons. It is illegal for a bondsperson to take a fee for putting up bail for you. In some major cities there are defence funds to assist you if you are a political person. These funds tend to specialize in helping people charged with drug or political offences but sometimes help other persons as well. There may be an organization in your area to assist you in raising your bail.

If you are charged with a summary offence, have not received bail within thirty days and your trial has not taken place, there is an onus in the Criminal Code on the gaoler in the gaol in which you are held to bring your case up for a review of your detention. The judge will either release you on bail and set an early trial date or else, if the prosecutor can satisfy the court why you should not be released, then expedite your trial date. In similar circumstances, if you have been held for ninety days for an indictable offence the gaoler must bring the case up before the judge and the judge will release you or set an early trial date or both.

One difficulty when bail is denied is that you may be unable to get in touch with witnesses who are drifters and may leave town before your trial if they don't know they are required. Alternatively, they may be in doubt as to whether or not they are required and will avoid making enquiries because of distrust of police. Whatever the case, contact them as soon as possible. If you can't reach them, give their names, addresses, and telephone numbers to your lawyer so that he or she can locate them and have them subpoenaed.

CHAPTER XII

SEARCH AND SEIZURE
UNDER THE WEAPONS LAWS

Canada's weapons laws are most sensible and more effective than those in the United States. The Canadian government takes a very dim view of individual citizens who arm themselves, except for the purpose of hunting game. No one has the right to keep a weapon for self-defence. Our neighbours in the United States have adopted a totally different theory. The American Bill of Rights guarantees the right of the people to keep and bear arms.

The matter of weapons is another area in which police have wide powers of search and seizure. The Criminal Code permits police to search, without a warrant, any person, vehicle, or place -- except a dwelling -- where they believe illegal weapons may be found. But, again, the law fails to give any guidance as to what sort of grounds a police officer needs to justify his or her belief.

If an officer stops you when you are driving and says he or she wishes to search your vehicle, ask on what authority the search is being made. If the officer does not say under the drug, liquor, or weapons laws, he or she has no right to make the search. If the search is being made under the drug laws, you may ask what drugs are being searched for. If the officer says he or she is making the search under the weapons law, you may ask what weapons are being searched for.

If there is no real point to the search, the officer may give up the idea when you make these requests. If, however, he or she states "all weapons," or "all drugs," and embarks upon the search with or without using force, there is little point in offering resistance. It is better to observe everything that the officer does and consult a lawyer before making any statements.

It is an offence to possess prohibited and restricted weapons. Prohibited weapons include arms with silencers, switchblade knives, restricted weapons, and any other weapon that is not a legal hunting weapon. Restricted weapons include handguns and any firearm less than twenty-six inches in length. Usually only bank robbers and antique gun collectors possess restricted weapons.

Buying, selling, giving, delivering, possessing, or lending a prohibited weapon is an indictable offence carrying a maximum penalty of five years although, in some instances, it may be dealt with summarily. Restricted weapons must be registered and you need a permit to take them anywhere. Police officials are usually in charge of registration.

Carrying or possessing a weapon, or an imitation of a weapon, for a purpose dangerous to the public peace, is also an offence.

What is a purpose dangerous to the public peace? Is possession of a weapon for a purpose of self-defence a purpose dangerous to the public peace? The courts have found so in cases where the evidence showed that the accused might have had to use it if a confrontation had been imminent. If you carry a hunting knife for protection when you travel, you could be charged. However, if the hunting knife was used for cutting meat or cleaning fish, you would probably not be charged.

There is some confusion about what qualifies as a weapon. The Criminal Code defines a weapon as anything that is designed to be used as a weapon or anything that a person uses or intends to use as a weapon. A butcher knife is an implement for cutting meat or bread until the person possessing it uses it for a weapon. If you threaten someone with a butcher knife, it becomes a weapon. If you carry a butcher knife to the scene of a riot and there is no food to cut, a court might find that the circumstances are sufficient to permit an inference that you intended to use it as a weapon.

CHAPTER XIII

DEMONSTRATIONS AND PROTESTS

Demonstrations and protests can be an effective method of educating people, and even attaining political goals. Freedom of assembly is guaranteed in the Canadian Bill of Rights. Police maintain a close guard upon any public assembly -- on the justification that the right to demonstrate or protest carries with it the responsibility of maintaining the public peace, which infers the sanctity of other people's property. Sometimes police will act justifiably to break up a demonstration. Sometimes they act without justification.

The presence of police at a demonstration is predictable. They may be in uniform, or in plainclothes, mingling with the demonstrators. Obviously, it is most unwise to be in possession of drugs, weapons, or alcohol during a demonstration.

If you have drugs in your possession, you will be charged. If you have a weapon, even a hunting knife, you may be charged with possession of a weapon for a dangerous purpose. Possession of alcohol may well bring charges.

Try to stay near one or more friends so that someone will know if you are arrested. Your friends should be able to get a lawyer and arrange bail. They will know what you were doing prior to the arrest and can testify at your trial. If a friend is arrested, try to get the badge numbers of the officers concerned, and the names of other witnesses.

If you are arrested, it is best to make no statements until you talk to a lawyer. If you are emotionally involved in a demonstration and its objectives, you may be tempted to make rash statements in the heat of the moment. You should resist this temptation. Anything you have said will be recorded as soon as the arresting officers have an opportunity and will be tendered against you in court. Police may ask for the names of persons accompanying you at the demonstration. If you give names, these persons may also be arrested and charged. If you are a juvenile, tell the police so at the earliest opportunity.

If you are wrongfully arrested during the course of a demonstration, you will probably be released later. There is little point in telling an officer who arrests you at a demonstration that you are innocent -- he or she will be much too busy doing his or her job and isn't going to take time out to deal with your individual case. If you resist arrest, you may possibly be charged with a more serious offence such as assaulting or obstructing a police officer.

If police officers act without justification, and tear into the crowd beating and arresting people, there will be lots of witnesses. Damage suits can be brought against the police in civil law for assault and battery or false arrest and imprisonment, or both. There may also be criminal charges of common assault laid against the officers. It is important to keep a cool head and observe what is going on around you. In court your recollection of exactly what happened may be crucial.

The most common charge used to break up a demonstration is that of causing a disturbance. This is a summary offence under the Criminal Code and carries a maximum penalty of six months' imprisonment, or a fine of $500, or both. You can cause a disturbance within the meaning of the code by fighting, shouting, swearing, singing, using insulting or obscene language, being drunk, loitering, impeding, obstructing, or molesting other persons. You may also be charged for an indecent exhibition, or disorderly conduct in a public place.

Another charge used to break up a demonstration is that of unlawful assembly. An unlawful assembly is a group of three or more persons who, with a common purpose, cause others to fear a serious disturbance of the peace. Being a member of an unlawful assembly is a summary offence carrying a maximum penalty of a $500 fine, or six months' imprisonment, or both.

A riot is an unlawful assembly that has begun to disturb the peace tumultuously. When a riot breaks out, a justice, mayor, sheriff, or deputy may read the Riot Proclamation which is as follows:

"Her Majesty the Queen charges and commands all persons being assembled immediately to disperse and peaceably to depart to their habitations or to their lawful business upon the pain of being guilty of an offence for which, upon conviction, they may be sentenced to imprisonment for life. God Save the Queen."

If you hear this proclamation read, SPLIT. The maximum penalty for failing to disperse within thirty minutes is life imprisonment. The same penalty holds for the offence of hindering the person making the proclamation. You must also leave within thirty minutes when you know there has been an unsuccessful attempt to read the proclamation. Participation in a riot is indictable and carries a maximum penalty of two years' imprisonment.

53

CHAPTER XIV

SEX AND THE LAW

Charges for sex and morals offences are comparatively rare. They usually come to light when police are watching people for an entirely different reason, or because of information received from informers.

A husband and wife, or two people over twenty-one years of age, may perform any sexual act in private if both consent. Such an act is not considered to be private if more than two persons are present or take part, or if it is conducted in a public place.

Cunnilingus is the oral contact by a male with female genitals. Fellatio is the oral contact by a female with male genitals. These acts are legal if performed in private by husband and wife or by consenting adults over twenty-one. If one or both persons are under twenty-one, both may be charged. If the act occurs in the presence of others, anyone who is involved may be charged. The probable charge is gross indecency, an indictable offence carrying a maximum penalty of five years' imprisonment.

If both parties are over twenty-one, and both consent, homosexual or lesbian sex in private is legal. Again, if one or both persons are under twenty-one, or if others are present, both participants may be charged with gross indecency. It is interesting to note how the law discriminates against "gay" people. Society condones varied sex acts for persons who are married, no matter how old they are. "Gays" are forbidden to marry and, therefore, must wait, legally, until they are twenty-one before "legally" engaging in homosexual acts.

Statutory rape is committed when a man has intercourse with a girl under the age of sixteen. He may be guilty of this offence even if he believed that she was sixteen or older. However, where the girl is between fourteen and sixteen, the man isn't guilty unless it can be proved that he was more to blame than the girl. The maximum penalty for having intercourse with a girl between fourteen and sixteen is five years. If the girl is under fourteen the maximum is life imprisonment.

If you have intercourse with a girl or boy under the juvenile age, which is sixteen, seventeen, or eighteen, depending upon the province in which it occurs, you may be charged with contributing to juvenile delinquency. Proof that intercourse with the juvenile did not make that person a delinquent is no defence, but there must be proof that you knew the person was a juvenile. If you believed he or she was over the juvenile age, you have a defence.

Most people believe that prostitution is illegal in Canada, but it would be nearer the truth to say that it isn't. Houses of prostitution are illegal. It is illegal for a girl to be an inmate of a bawdy house. Pimping is illegal, but we have no law which covers call-girls. Even street prostitution, strictly speaking, is not illegal. It is illegal to solicit a person in a public place for the purpose of prostitution. This is a summary offence punishable by six months in gaol, or a $500 fine, or both.

Soliciting is the commonest kind of charge relating to prostitution and one supposes it is used to keep the streets orderly. Under the old law, known prostitutes could be challenged under the vagrancy "C" section of the Criminal Code, which has been repealed, and required to give a good account of themselves. Under the new law, police must actually have evidence of soliciting and men as well as women can be charged with soliciting. The section is not restricted to women as it was under the previous law. The word solicit in the dictionary means "ask, seek earnestly or pleadingly, beg or entreat such as in, "We solicit your support," or "He solicited them for help." A second meaning is to tempt or entice another person to do wrong. A third definition is to accost another person for some immoral purpose such as a prostitute does. Prostitution refers to the selling of the services of oneself or another for the purpose of sexual intercourse. It means to sell one's artistic or moral integrity

for a low or unworthy purpose or to be given over to base
purposes. The noun "prostitute" refers, in its first meaning, to a woman who engages in promiscuous sexual intercourse for pay. Alternate words are "whore" and "harlot."

Clearly it is the person who makes the solicitation for
the purpose of prostitution who can be found guilty of this
offence. One wonders what the situation is where a man
approaches a prostitute and proposes prostitution to her. Is
he guilty of soliciting her for the purpose of prostitution?
This has not as yet been resolved but it seems unlikely
that the courts would go this far.

A man arrested in a house of prostitution or a bawdy
house can be charged as a found-in. Under the former law,
a man found with a woman in a vagrancy "C" situation
could not be prosecuted. It seems very unlikely that a man
could be prosecuted under the soliciting section of the Criminal Code.

It is also illegal in our law to be nude in a public place or on private property if you are in public view. The word "nude" is defined in the Criminal Code as being "so clad as to offend against public decency or order." The law doesn't give any standard of public decency or suggest what offends public order. Nudity is a summary offence and the consent of the provincial Attorney-General must be obtained before any prosecution can be started. This particular bureaucratic requirement is probably one reason why the nudity charge is not used more often.

CHAPTER XV

BOOKED, FINGERPRINTED, AND PHOTOGRAPHED

We have seen that police have a right to search a person they have arrested. They will search for weapons which might be used to assist an escape or to commit suicide, or for evidence relating to the charge against you. This search usually occurs at the time of booking and it may include a skin-frisk. If, in the process, they find evidence, such as drugs, to support another completely unrelated charge, you will have two charges booked against you.

At the booking desk the booking officer will take your personal possessions and will ask you to sign a paper listing them. He or she may chat about your arrest and may ask questions, but you are not required to talk or to answer the questions. Any police officer to whom you make incriminating statements may be called as a witness against you. If you want to be friendly, talk about the weather, the condition of the cells or the food, but **don't** talk about your charge.

Stool pigeons are sometimes planted in cells with persons who have been arrested. This is a sure-fire method of getting voluntary confessions. Prisoners often chat about what they're in for; some like to boast about their particular exploit. An inflated boast to an undercover officer could convict an innocent accused. For your own self-preservation, you should be friendly to cell-mates, but **don't** talk about your case.

If you have been improperly arrested for something that you did not do and for which you are certain there is no evidence, this may be the time to bring it up to the gaol guards. You can tell the officers that you believe you are the wrong person to be charged and request to see the officer-in-charge. It cannot be emphasized too much that it is much better to consult with a lawyer before doing this. However, in some circumstances, such as where you are arrested for being drunk in a public place and had had nothing to drink, a request to see the officer-in-charge and an interview with him or her may effect your release much sooner than any other strategy.

If at this time you haven't been released by the arresting officer or the officer-in-charge, you can request to see a justice or a justice of the peace on the matter of getting released. Or, you can ask to see the officer-in-charge if you have not requested release from him or her and if you are eligible for a release by an officer-in-charge. A justice of the peace can release an accused for any but the most serious of offences. However, there are usually no provincial court judges or magistrates sitting on Saturday night and Sunday which means that if you are arrested on Saturday afternoon you may be kept in custody until Monday morning until your detention is reviewed by a judge. In most large centres there are justices available twenty-four hours a day who will review your detention at any time.

You have a right to make telephone calls to notify relatives and to obtain counsel. Your right to counsel is guaranteed in the Canadian Bill of Rights. Police cannot refuse you the right to make reasonable efforts to contact a lawyer of your choice. If they refuse to grant you access to a telephone, wait until you get a chance to go into the courtroom, then bring it to the attention of the judge who will order that you are to be allowed a phone call immediately.

In most cases where you are charged with an offence carrying a maximum gaol term of five years or less, you will be released by the arresting officer or by the officer-in-charge. It is only where they have grounds for believing that you will not show up for your court appearances that they will keep you in custody. Otherwise, you will probably be released on a simple appearance notice, promise to appear, or summons. Where you are arrested on the ground that you were about to commit an indictable offence, you will be released unconditionally once police are satisfied that you will not commit the offence. If they do not release you, they must take you before a justice of the peace, provincial court judge, or magistrate within twenty-four hours.

The Identification of Criminals Act gives police a right to fingerprint and photograph persons charged with an indictable offence. They may use force if necessary. It should be remembered that many drug and weapons charges may be either summary or indictable at the option of the prosecutor. All these offences should be treated as indictable. If you resist fingerprinting and photographing on a charge such as possession of marihuana, the prosecutor may decide to proceed by indictable offence, if for no other reason than to protect the police who may have forcibly fingerprinted and photographed you.

Where you are charged with a summary offence, police have no right to take fingerprints and photographs. You are entitled to resist. If the police use force, you may sue civilly for damages or lay a charge of common assault.

If you are released on an appearance notice, promise to appear, or recognizance, you can be required by that document to appear at a specified time and place for fingerprinting and photographing. If you do not appear at the time and place specified for these purposes, a warrant can be issued for your arrest for the offence with which you are charged. This means that the form of bail that is in effect will be cancelled and you will be held in custody unless there is a new undertaking, promise to appear, or recognizance.

CHAPTER XVI

BEFORE THE TRIAL

The first preparation you will need to make for your trial is to obtain the services of a lawyer. Even if you are thinking of pleading guilty to a summary offence, for example, possession of marihuana, it may still be useful to speak with a lawyer first. The law is very complex and it is sometimes difficult for a layperson to defend himself or herself in the criminal courts. There may be defences open to you that you have not thought of. For example, it is possible that you may be in possession of a drug physically but may not have known that the drug was in the particular location in which it was found on your person, or that it was the particular drug which it is alleged to be. You should consult a lawyer on these matters.

We have already seen that you have a right to counsel which is guaranteed in the Canadian Bill of Rights. If you can't afford a lawyer, apply for legal aid. To find out about legal aid, contact the nearest Salvation Army post, the John Howard or Elizabeth Fry Societies, the local Bar association or law society office or ask the judge about legal aid. If you cannot get legal aid and you cannot afford a lawyer, ask the judge for a court-appointed lawyer. Everyone has the right to legal counsel on a criminal charge.

In Canada there is no guarantee of an early trial date. If, for whatever reason, you want an early trial, you must bring it to the attention of the court at the time a trial date is being set. In the United States the Second Amendment to the American Bill of Rights guarantees the right to a speedy and public trial by jury. We do not have such a guarantee in our Canadian Bill of Rights.

The only provision that the Criminal Code has with regard to the obtaining of an early trial date are in circumstances where the accused is still in custody and the trial is delayed. As we have already seen, where an accused is still in custody thirty days after the date of his or her first court appearance on a summary offence, or ninety days after the date of the first court offence on an indictable offence, the person having custody of the accused, or the gaoler, must apply to a judge for a hearing to determine whether the accused should be released. In this hearing the judge will take into consideration whether the delay has been caused by the accused or the prosecutor and will decide whether the continued detention of the accused is justified. The judge may also give directions for expediting the trial of the accused.

You can get a copy of the charge against you from the office of the court clerk. You also have a right to know the particulars of the prosecutor's allegations against you. You may obtain particulars informally by telephone, or by a written demand to the prosecutor. If you have a lawyer, he or she will do this for you. The particulars must be sufficient to inform you of the specific allegations against you.

For example, if you are arrested, along with two or three other people, in a house in which three or four caches of drugs are found, you are entitled to know what particular drugs have been found and which drugs you are charged with possessing. You are entitled to know how much of any particular drug was found, in what form of packaging it was found, and precisely where it was found.

If you do not get sufficient particulars, tell the judge when you applied for them and ask him or her to order the prosecutor to supply the information. You may also ask for an adjournment to prepare your defence.

The term "arraignment" means appearing before the trial judge and pleading to the charge. If you are charged with an indictable offence, you may have an option to be tried by magistrate, higher court judge, or judge and jury. If you elect trial by higher court judge and jury, the magistrate will hold a preliminary hearing. You will be brought to the bar to plead, or be arraigned, in the higher court. If, however, you elect trial by magistrate, your arraignment will usually follow immediately, with the clerk of the court reading the charge again and asking whether you plead "guilty" or "not guilty."

A few indictable offences **must** be tried by a magistrate or provincial court judge. The common offences which fall within this rule are: resisting or obstructing a police officer, assault causing bodily harm, assault on a police officer, driving while disqualified from driving, theft under $200, false pretences under $200, possession of stolen property under $200, bookmaking, and keeping a bawdy house. In addition, all summary offences are tried only before a magistrate. In these cases you have no election and no right to preliminary hearing.

Your election and plea may be very important to your defence. You should discuss these matters with your lawyer before committing yourself to a course of action. If the court asks you to elect or plead before you have counsel or before you have discussed this with your lawyer, ask for a one-week adjournment to obtain counsel or discuss the matter with your counsel. There may be many cases in which it is important to have a preliminary hearing to see what the Crown's evidence is against you.

At the preliminary hearing, the prosecutor will parade his or her witnesses who will give their evidence against you. You or your lawyer have the right to cross-examine the witnesses. At the termination of the prosecutor's evidence, you also have the right to call witnesses or give evidence, or you can simply make a statement to the court without taking the witness box if you wish. This is not done very often and a preliminary hearing is used by defence counsel only for the purpose of hearing the prosecutor's evidence. At the termination of the enquiry, if the evidence is weak, your lawyer can make a motion for your discharge from custody on the basis that there is insufficient evidence to commit you for trial. The prosecutor does not have to have evidence beyond a reasonable doubt at the preliminary hearing; it is sufficient if he or she can show a case of probable guilt.

There is no new bail set if you are committed for trial. The bail which was set at the outset of your case will continue unless there are changed circumstances or new charges. In high court, arraignment occurs on the date of the trial. If there is a jury, you are arraigned in the presence of the jury.

A brief word should be said here about plea bargaining. Plea bargaining refers to a situation where the prosecutor compromises with the defence lawyer to arrange the settlement of one or several charges. For example, if you are charged with possession of marihuana for the purpose of trafficking and are intending to plead not guilty and the case is set for trial, the prosecutor may wish to avoid a trial and may be willing to accept a plea to a straight charge of possession rather than possession for the purpose of trafficking. If this is done, the prosecutor would stay the proceedings or withdraw the charge of possession for the purpose of trafficking and lay a new charge of simple possession to which you would plead guilty.

Plea bargaining occurs all the time; it is obviously an efficient manner in which the prosecutor can deal with a large number of charges against one person. It is **usually** beneficial to the accused if he or she has a good defence to all the charges. You should never consider any form of plea bargaining with police. Police have no right to bind the prosecutor or the judge. Nor can anyone bind the judge as far as sentence goes. There can be no plea bargaining in respect of sentence. If a police officer or a prosecutor indicates to you that you may get a suspended sentence for pleading guilty to a charge, you should not talk further. Neither can guarantee that the judge will give you a suspended sentence in return for a plea of guilty. It is true that judges often consider the fact of a plea of guilty and the fact that it has saved the court and the taxpayers money. However, they are not bound to consider this and it is only one of many factors that they may consider in settling a sentence.

It is important to point out that the prosecutor may decide at any time to stay the proceedings in a case against you. A stay of proceedings is exactly what it says -- an arrest of the proceedings. They can be started again. In point of fact, proceedings are usually stayed when there is no evidence on which to proceed or where a plea bargain has been struck with defence counsel. This means that cases in which there has been a stay of proceedings entered are seldom heard from again. It is important to note that a stay of proceedings is not the same as an acquittal. It is, in fact, a postponement, delay, or temporary arrest of the case. The **stay of proceedings has, unfortunately, nothing to do with the** judge but can be arbitrarily exercised by the prosecutor. The prosecutor can do it in any case. This means that in the case of any indictable offence, you have no right to be ulti-mately proven innocent because the prosecutor can enter a stay of proceedings rather than have a trial.*

In the author's opinion, this is a section of the criminal law which should be changed so that an accused has a right to be proved innocent if he or she wishes.

CHAPTER XVII

THE COURSE OF TRIAL

You are presumed innocent in a criminal trial until the prosecutor proves your guilt beyond a reasonable doubt. A reasonable doubt is a doubt based upon reason or logic. It cannot be a fanciful or imaginary doubt, but must arise from evidence given in the trial.

The following examples are indicative of the "guilt beyond a reasonable doubt" principle. The examples given deal with narcotics charges, which are very common, but the principle of proving guilt beyond a reasonable doubt in any criminal charge is well exemplified.

Suppose you are a passenger in the front seat of a car which is stopped and searched for narcotics. Police find an ounce of marihuana in the glove compartment. The driver and yourself remain silent. The court may find that there is some evidence that the driver, or owner, of the car knew the drug was there. The driver or owner must raise a reasonable doubt bout his or her knowledge of drugs being present in the car.

As a passenger you would be acquitted because the prosecutor would be unable to establish that you knew the drug was there. There would be more than a reasonable doubt in your case. Indeed, there would be no case to answer. The prosecutor needs more evidence than this to establish possession.

Take another case. A girl is arrested by two male officers on a charge of possession of narcotics. (Remember that male officers, even after a legal arrest, have no right to search a female accused.) They drive her back to the station to be searched by a police matron. When they take her out of the paddy wagon, a small piece of scrunched-up foil is found in the wagon and found to contain hash. She doesn't have any drugs on her person but is charged with possession of the hash found in the wagon. At her trial, police testify they didn't see the tin foil in the wagon before she was put into it. In these circumstances there is some evidence against her, but not enough to prove her guilt beyond a reasonable doubt.

There is no evidence that she put the drug in the wagon and nothing to tie the piece of tin foil to her, other than the fact that the police say it didn't appear to be in the wagon when they loaded her into it. The doubt raised upon such evidence is a question of whether the tin foil containing the hash could have been in the wagon from some other source.

It may be dangerous to give evidence in a case of this sort. By taking the witness stand to deny putting the drug in the wagon, your credibility is placed in issue. If the judge doesn't believe you, he or she may convict.

Suppose you have just left your home and you are wearing your room-mate's coat. An RCMP officer stops you and advises you that he or she has reasonable and probable grounds for believing you are in possession of a narcotic and then proceeds to search you under the Narcotic Control Act. In the course of the search, the officer produces a lid of grass from the pocket of the coat you are wearing. You did not know it was there. Your obvious defence is that the coat was your room-mate's and he or she hadn't told you that the drug was in it. What can you do in these circumstances?

In your defence, your room-mate may testify, under the protection of the Canada Evidence Act, that it is his or her jacket, his or her drug, and when you borrowed the jacket he or she forgot to tell you about the presence of the drug. You should also give the same evidence.

If the judge believes the evidence, or entertains a doubt as to whether it is true or false, you will be acquitted.

Perhaps you are living in a communal house when police enter with a writ of assistance and find a kilogram of marihuana concealed in a broom closet located in a central hallway. Without confessions, the police are helpless.

They cannot tie the marihuana to a particular person in order to satisfy the legal requirements of possession. The marihuana will be seized and destroyed but, in all probability, no one will be charged.

If, however, it can be proved that one person rented the place, that person may be charged. If it can be proved that only one person had belongings in the broom closet, that person may be charged. Even in this case, however, acquittal is very probable because the prosecutor must prove the case beyond a reasonable doubt, and if there should be a possibility that more than one person had access to the closet, someone other than the person charged may have owned the drugs and hidden them there. This would create a reasonable doubt.

Suppose your case is set for trial and the prosecutor requests an adjournment because a witness isn't available. If you are ready for trial, you may move for dismissal of the case for want of prosecution. If you or your witnesses would be inconvenienced by a further delay of the trial by, say, losing job opportunities, tell the judge about it. A judge is much more likely to dismiss a summary offence, in these circumstances, than an indictable offence.

The Criminal Code guarantees your right to be present throughout your trial. However, if you interrupt the proceedings to the extent that continuation of the trial is no longer feasible, the court may have you removed. Remember the plight of Bobby Seale at the Chicago Seven conspiracy trial where this very thing happened.*

Your right to a fair trial is supplemented by certain provisions in the Criminal Code. For example, one provision gives you the right to make full answer and defence to the charge against you and you have this right even if your defence is ridiculous. The judge must hear it out. If the judge refuses to do so, you may have good grounds for appeal. You also have the right to cross-examine the prosecution witnesses. At the end of your evidence, you may sum up your case and make a legal argument to the judge.

*During a part of the case, Seale was bound and gagged by the court officers when the judge decided he was unduly interrupting the proceedings.

The comments of a judge during a trial should relate only to the proceedings and the evidence before him or her, not to the color of your skin, or the cut of your clothes. However, in the courtroom, the judge is supreme and has a wide power of discretion as to what he or she will allow. Unfortunately, judges are not gods; they are human beings, subject to the same personal idiosyncracies as all of us. It is for this reason that one judge will react in a very bitter and rude manner to a person clad in a manner he or she disapproves of, whereas another judge will not react in the slightest to the appearance of the person before him or her. Most judges are above this sort of comment. They realize that members of the public are not too well acquainted with the courtrooms. If a person violates the decor of the court-room by smoking a cigarette, the usual and predictable reac-tion of a provincial court judge will be to tell the person to put it out. Smoking is prohibited in the courtroom. There are, however, some judges who will immediately ask the person to show cause why they should not be cited for a contempt in the face of the court. This is obviously a very bad thing in that the average person's total interaction with the law may be one appearance in provincial court. One can get a bad impression if the wrong judge is presiding.

It is quite impossible to detail every circumstance in which you may justifiably apply for a mistrial, but whenever a judge makes a grave procedural error, such as denying the right to cross-examine a witness, or to give evidence, thereby indicating prejudice or bias against you, then you may have grounds. A motion for mistrial is a request to the judge to declare the proceedings a mistrial.

It is always prudent to be as polite as possible to the judge. If you have a defence and must go in a witness box to give evidence, you will want to be believed. It will hurt your chances if you are striking a discordant relationship with the judge. He or she ultimately has a lot of power in deciding whether or not the evidence you give in court should be believed.

You must also remember that judges have a contempt power. If you commit a contempt in the face of the court, such as by throwing a paper cup at the judge, you will probably be convicted summarily for contempt of court and a punishment will be immediately imposed. You have a right to appeal from the conviction, or from the punishment, or from both. A more serious contempt, such as public ridicule of the judge, can lead to an indictable charge against you.

CHAPTER XVIII

DISCHARGES, CONVICTIONS, AND SENTENCES

A judge can find a person guilty without convicting him or her. Similarly, a person who pleads guilty may not be convicted. Wherever the offence is one punishable by a maximum penalty of less than fourteen years (including theft under $200, false pretences, possession of stolen property, all drug possession charges, weapons charges, charges of skipping bail, escaping custody, causing a disturbance, unlawful assembly, soliciting, impaired driving, driving while disqualified, hit and run, assaulting a police officer, common assault, obstructing or resisting a police officer and assault causing bodily harm) the court may discharge the accused absolutely or conditionally instead of convicting him or her. The effect of an absolute discharge is that the accused, although found guilty of the offence, walks out of the courtroom with no conviction and no penalty. The court can also impose a conditional discharge wherein there will be a probation order and the accused will be directed to comply with the conditions of the probation order. The effect of this discharge is that the accused is deemed not to have been convicted of the offence to which he or she pleaded or was found guilty.

The conditional and absolute discharges are curious additions to our criminal law. Can a person who gets a conditional discharge honestly say he or she has no criminal record? Or can that person only say that he or she has no convictions? The traditional approach is that a person does not have a criminal record unless convicted of a criminal offence. Therefore, it would seem logical that the people who have been discharged have not been convicted and, therefore, have no criminal record. This would be the best approach for a discharged person to take. Potential employers with whom a discharged person may come into contact may not fully appreciate the impact of a technicality that Parliament has passed into law. It is better to tell them you have no criminal record, if you must comment on it at all.

It is clear that the discharge situation has been invoked to stem or control the great rising tide of "criminals" resulting from violations of the narcotics laws. The use of marihuana, hashish, and others of the soft drugs is now so widespread that it hits every corner, segment, and level of our society. Perhaps the sons and daughters of parliamentarians and even some of the parliamentarians themselves have been using these drugs and felt it was time to take appropriate steps to ensure that illegal possession of these drugs would not necessarily result in a conviction. This is the effect of the measure which they have taken. They have not legalized marihuana and hashish, but they have given the courts a method by which they can avoid convicting violators. It indirectly achieves the same thing as legalization of marihuana.

Once you have been convicted of an offence, you will be sentenced by the judge. If you are youthful or if it is your first offence, there will probably be a probation report and, if the crime of which you were convicted is not aggravated, you will likely be given a discharge, if eligible, or a suspended sentence and placed on probation for a period up to three years. In appropriate cases, fines will be imposed or short terms of gaol. For certain offences a gaol term is almost a certainty. The Criminal Code now has provisions for intermittent gaol sentences where the total amount of imprisonment does not exceed ninety days. This means that a person who is going to school could continue to go to school on the week days and serve the gaol term on the weekends. It is probably a good move because, formerly, persons who were sent to gaol were forced to isolate and cut themselves off completely from the activities in the community. Now they can continue to support their families and / or pursue their career or education while serving the gaol term. Probbably people who are engaged in doing any of those things shouldn't be gaoled in the first place, but our society still has to go a long way before it will accept that premise.

CHAPTER XIX

CRIMINAL RECORDS

Any conviction under the Criminal Code, Narcotic Control Act, or Food and Drug Act will give you a criminal record. No distinction is made between a summary and an indictable offence. The record is tied to you by your name, a number, and your fingerprints and photographs, if they have been taken.

If you have been acquitted, do the RCMP maintain a record of your case? Yes, they do.

Technically, a charge doesn't give you a criminal record unless it results in a conviction. For court purposes, a charge which results in an acquittal doesn't count but, for RCMP investigative purposes, a charge is equal to a conviction. The RCMP Identification Branch in Ottawa will tell you that only convictions are on your record and that if you don't have a conviction you don't have a record. This is not true.

For example, suppose that you have been arrested for, say, possession of marihuana and have been fingerprinted and photographed. This information -- the fact that you were charged with possession of marihuana, the date and place of trial, and the result of the trial -- is recorded and kept on file in Ottawa. You were acquitted of the charge but a year later you are stopped by police for, say, driving too slowly. The officer checks your driver's licence, registration, and insurance, but becomes suspicious because you appear nervous. The officer then asks to search the car and you ask what for. He or she is unable to state a reason and is ready to give up the attempt, but radios to headquarters for a warrant check and, at the same time, may get an identification check to see whether you have a record. If the officer finds out that you were previously charged with possession of a drug, he or she will press the search, even though you were acquitted.

In court a criminal record will affect your position on bail applications, making it more than likely that high bail will be sought. It will also affect your position when sentence is passed. Logically, there is no justification for getting a heavier sentence on conviction for causing a disturbance if you have a previous record for, say, possession of a narcotic, or for some other unrelated offence, but the judge will probably be influenced by the fact that you have a previous record.

A criminal record has other disadvantages. It may well affect your chances when you apply for certain jobs, particularly those where you are required to be bonded. It can also hurt when you apply for any job if the potential employer becomes aware of it.

If you are a Canadian citizen, a criminal record does not affect your right to a Canadian passport although it may affect your right to enter foreign countries. If you are a citizen of another country applying to enter Canada, a criminal record may prevent you from gaining landed immigrant status. If you are a landed immigrant, a conviction may hinder your application for citizenship.

The Prisons Records Act enables you to apply for a pardon from a summary conviction two years after the sentence is served, i.e., when a period of probation or term of imprisonment expires, or when a fine is paid, whichever happens last. For indictable convictions, you must wait five years for pardon.

The Criminal Records Act also applies to a person who has been granted an absolute or conditional discharge. Where a discharge is granted in respect of a summary offence, an application for pardon may be made one year after the date on which the discharge was granted in the case of an absolute discharge and one year from the date of termination of the period of probation in the case of a conditional discharge. In the case of indictable offences, you must wait three years for one of these two events to occur.

CHAPTER XX

JUVENILES IN THE CRIMINAL LAW

The age at which a juvenile may be charged in adult court varies from province to province. In Saskatchewan, Ontario, New Brunswick, and the Territories, it is sixteen. In British Columbia, it is seventeen. In Manitoba and Quebec, it is eighteen. In Alberta, boys may be charged in adult court if they are sixteen, but girls must be eighteen.

These ages apply to young people who are charged with offences, but the provinces have other laws respecting young people. Each province may set a different age at which you can drive a motor vehicle, make a legal contract, smoke cigarettes, see raunchy movies, or drink alcohol. If you want information about any of these regulations you should write to the Attorney-General or the Justice Minister of your province or consult legal aid sources.

Curiously, you could be arraigned in adult court on a charge of being a minor in possession of liquor. The adult court age is usually lower than the drinking age. This doesn't make any sense. It is like being drafted for military service before you are old enough to vote for or against the war.

Juvenile crime is governed by the Juvenile Delinquents Act which contains only one offence -- the offence of delinquency. Delinquency may mean anything from skipping school to armed robbery.

Charges in juvenile court usually read as follows:

"Jane Youngman is charged that she did, on the 5th day of March, 1975, in the City of Toronto, in the Province of Ontario, commit the offence of delinquency; to wit, jaywalking."

Delinquency covers any violation of a provincial statute, a city by-law, or a provision of the Criminal Code or other federal act, including the Food and Drug Act and the Narcotic Control Act.

One kind of delinquency is sexual immorality "or any similar form of vice." If you are a juvenile girl and you have intercourse with an adult boyfriend, it seems your parents could complain to the juvenile authorities and have you charged with delinquency. They could also have your boyfriend charged with contributing, or, if you are under sixteen, with statutory rape.

The laws for arrest, search, and seizure for juveniles are the same as for adult offencers. Nevertheless, as indicated earlier, if you are arrested, you should inform the authorities of your legal age as soon as possible. Tell the police or the court. They must then transfer you to juvenile court.

When you are registered at the detention home, provide the name, telephone number, and address of your parents. The juvenile court authorities will call them. If they do not do so, request a telephone call and ask your parents to come to where you are. Unless the alleged offence is very serious, you will be released into the custody of your parents.

In juvenile court you do not have a statutory right to appear before a justice or judge within twenty-four hours but, in practice, you will appear within twenty-four hours, or as soon after your arrest as a judge is sitting.

If your parents are in court, the judge will probably order your release into their custody without bail. If your parents are "no-goods" the court may release you into the custody of the Children's Aid Society, or keep you in the detention home. The court has the power to set bail in the same way an adult court does, but will usually avoid doing so unless the offence is serious and there is a possibility that you may skip bail. If you are charged with being a runaway, you will probably be held in a detention home until your hearing, or until your parents come to collect you.

A juvenile cannot be fingerprinted or photographed. A delinquent is regarded as a person needing guidance and help, not as a criminal. The offence of delinquency isn't, technically, a crime; it is a state of being. A juvenile record isn't a criminal record. A charge of delinquency, even if it would be an indictable offence in adult court, is not a crime in juvenile court.

Juveniles may get legal aid in most provinces, but it is restricted to cases where the outcome may be imprisonment in a training school, or transfer to adult court. Legal aid will be denied if your parents can afford a lawyer.

Arraignment is different in juvenile court. You have no right to jury trial, and no election. You do not plead guilty or not guilty. The charge will be read to you and you will be asked if you admit or deny the allegation of delinquency.

Your trial should be a fair one in accordance with the Bill of Rights, but, unless you have a lawyer, your rights may not be honored. Juvenile courts are overloaded, and the court officials tend to be in a hurry. The rules of evidence are relaxed. The judge may allow hearsay evidence to be given, which is something that could not be done in adult court.

The maximum fine a juvenile court can impose is twenty-five dollars. It may make a probation order, or merely suspend sentence without order. It may sentence you to a period of incarceration in a training institution, but will only do so in serious cases, or where there is a past record of delinquency.

If you are charged with a serious offence, such as trafficking in drugs, you are fortunate to be a juvenile. If you have a good home, you may get probation and be left in the custody of your parents. If it is the second time you have been caught, or if you have a bad record, you may be sent to a training school. In adult court you would get a term of imprisonment for a similar offence.

If your home is bad, you may be turned over to the Children's Aid Society, or to its counterpart, the Catholic Family and Children's Service.

Juvenile courts have the power to transfer you to adult court. You are eligible for transfer if you are fourteen and if the alleged delinquency would be indictable in adult court. Usually the transfer is initiated on the advice of a probation officer. If the alleged delinquency is serious, such as trafficking in a narcotic, or, if you have been on probation previously by order of the juvenile court, and if you are close to the age at which you become a legal adult in a particular province, the probation officer may recommend such a transfer and the juvenile court judge will order a hearing at which the probation officer will testify. His or her evidence may form the main part of the prosecutor's case.

The prosecutor must prove that it is in the interests of you and the community that you be tried in an adult court. In effect, it must be proved that the juvenile court can't help you.

CHAPTER XXI

WIRETAPPING LAW EXPLAINED

The Federal Government has now legalized wiretapping by police in Canada. Under a new law which became effective June 30, 1974, Parliament provided a legal means by which law enforcement authorities can intercept, listen to, and record conversations, or any other kind of oral communication or telecommunication. The interception of private communications through wiretapping and other devices has always been carried on by the RCMP and other police and law enforcement agencies in Canada. However, in the past, because it was obviously an invasion of privacy, a kind of trespass, and was thought to be illegal (and in fact, from 1960, probably was illegal under the Bill of Rights), the police usually denied wiretapping existed. Only in cases where they sought to introduce tape recordings in evidence did they admit wiretapping.

Illegal wiretapping was used most often against political dissenters and those involved in organized crime. Police were able to "bug" whomever they wanted to regardless of time or place, and at their own discretion. There is no reason to suspect that the new wiretap law will change this since it will be enforced by the same police who have been doing illegal wiretaps. It will mean only that police needn't be so clandestine, since in many cases they will now have legal authorization from a judge to wiretap.

Many people were led to believe that the new wiretap bill would liberalize the law. In fact, because previously wiretapping was illegal, the legalization of wiretapping cannot possibly be expected to do so. However, if a police officer (or anyone else) intercepts a private communication illegally, he or she can be prosecuted. The maximum penalty for illegal interception is five years in jail; for illegally using or disclosing the private communication or part of it, or the fact of its existence, the maximum penalty is two years.

Where a person is convicted of one of these offences, the victim of the illegal wiretap can get an order that the felon pay up to $5,000 in damages. Possession, sale or purchase of any electromagnetic, acoustic, or mechanical device that is primarily used for unauthorized interception of private communications is also an indictable offence, carrying a maximum penalty of two years.

The Federal Government left some important loopholes for illegal wiretappers. For example, the new laws provide that no legal authorization to wiretap is needed where one of the parties to the communication consents to its being recorded. This would include an undercover officer. If an undercover officer were one of the people involved in the communication -- either as an originator of it, or as a receiver of it -- then he or she could consent to interception or recording of the communication. In this instance, the conversation would be admissible against the other party in court, even though it was obtained without a lawful authorization. Also, the police involved in interception would be immune to prosecution under the provisions of the wiretap law.

The new law allows prosecutors to use tape recordings of private conversations as evidence in criminal trials. Notice of intention to do this, along with a transcript of the alleged conversations, must be given to the accused person a reasonable time prior to the trial.

A superficial benefit of the new law is that a wiretapped conversation cannot be evidence unless it has been legally obtained. However, the law also provides that the judge may overlook a defect or irregularity in procedure in deciding whether the transcript of the wiretapped conversation is admissible in evidence. It remains to be seen as to how widely or narrowly the judges will construe this legal loophole. Also, if an undercover agent is party to the conversations, he or she may consent to the evidence being tendered. Privileged communications, that is, conversations between lawyers and their clients, will be inadmissible, as they have always been, unless they are in furtherance of a crime.

At the end of each year, the Solicitor-General of Canada must prepare a report of all wiretap authorizations. In addition, the provincial Attorney-General or the Solicitor-General must notify persons whom they have wiretapped within ninety days after the wiretap was removed.

To do a legal wiretap, police must obtain an authorization from a superior court judge. The application for a wiretap authorization must be signed by a provincial Attorney-General or the Solicitor-General of Canada, and the law provides that police must prove to the judge that other methods of investigation will fail. It remains to be seen whether the courts will require the police to prove this, or whether they will grant authorizations on the mere statement by police that a wiretap is necessary.

An authorization can allow police to wiretap and record telephone conversations, or use other methods of electronic surveillance, employing electromagnetic, acoustic, mechanical, or other devices. The authorization must state the offence, the type of communication to be intercepted, and the identity of the persons whose communications will be intercepted. The wiretap authorization is valid for thirty days and can be renewed for thirty days. The documents filed to obtain an authorization are secret and must be placed by the judge in a sealed packet.

Legal wiretapping is limited to cases where indictable offences are alleged. That is, wiretapping cannot be authorized for investigation of summary offences, such as common assault or causing a disturbance. The statute legalizing wiretaps, the Protection of Privacy Act, mentions certain indictable offences for which authorizations to wiretap will be granted. They include sedition, treason, intimidating Parliament, forging passports (making or dealing in them), hijacking, unlawful possession or use of explosives (including grenades), bribery of public officials (for example, judges, politicians, or police), acceptance of bribes by public officials, perjury, murder, kidnapping, distributing hate literature, robbery, extortion, breaking and entering, possession of stolen property, forgery, uttering (passing off forged documents, counterfeit money, etc. as genuine), theft from mail, threatening, bribing an agent, arson, counterfeiting, and theft over $200.

Police can also legally wiretap when making investigations under the Narcotic Control Act of allegations of trafficking, possession for the purpose of trafficking, importing, and exporting narcotics. They can also obtain authorizations to wiretap for investigations into drug trafficking under the Food and Drug Act and for the offences of unlawfully buying, making, or selling spirits under the Excise Act. The legal wiretap is available for any other indictable offence investigation if police can show the offence is part of a pattern of a conspiracy or organized crime.

Any conspiracy or attempt to commit any of these offences could be investigated by a legal wiretap. In addition, offences of illegal wiretapping or illegal possession of devices or equipment for illegal, surreptitious interception of private communications can also be investigated by legal wiretaps. It is hard to imagine, however, one division of the police using a legal wiretap to investigate illegal wiretapping by another division of the same police force. There are obviously big problems in enforcing the act, or in discovering whether it has been enforced.

POSTSCRIPT ONE

POWERS OF POLICE OFFICERS

It is important to realize that the police are protected by the law when they are acting lawfully. If they are doing something that they are authorized by law to do, such as making a legal arrest, they are justified in using as much force as is necessary to effect their lawful purpose provided that they act on reasonable and probable grounds. Police are allowed to use force in making the arrest unless it is shown that the arrest could have been effected by reasonable means in a less violent manner. They are also entitled to use handcuffs when they are reasonable in the circumstances for preventing a possible escape of the persons in custody. The acts of the police to choke a person suspected of having swallowed a capsule of heroin have also been justified by the law in Canada on the ground that the police officer has information reasonably justifying a belief that the accused is carrying a narcotic in his or her mouth. This is one law which clearly ought to be changed especially because possession of a narcotic for personal use is only a summary offence.

POSTSCRIPT TWO

POLICE MISCONDUCT -- THE USE OF
ILLEGALLY OBTAINED EVIDENCE IN CANADIAN COURTS

You can be convicted on illegally obtained evidence. Even if police grossly misconduct themselves, for example, by beating you to effect a search, you are not entitled to an acquittal if you are charged as a result of something found during the search. If the evidence is relevant to the charge against you, it is admissible. This runs against the trend of American law where the court tends to require observance of due process during all stages of your case, including arrest and search.

Canadian law in this respect is somewhat hypocritical. Our laws set certain requirements for legal arrest, search, and seizure. In contrast, our courts don't enforce these laws and permit the use of illegally obtained evidence. Police won't stop using illegal methods if they can use the evidence against you in court. It seems pathetic that the criminal courts, which should be the guardians of due process, allow police to bring illegally obtained evidence before them. The question could be asked, "Why has no Canadian court applied our Bill of Rights to exclude evidence obtained as a result of an illegal arrest or search?"

Police in Canada can now use electronic eavesdropping equipment legally. See the chapter entitled "Wiretapping Law Explained" for further details.

Illegal methods are used to obtain evidence in drug cases. Undercover officers masquerading as users often induce suspects to sell illegal drugs. In effect, police are permitted to commit the offence of counselling another to commit an offence.

There is a potential defence of entrapment. It is applied in the United States where the accused would not have committed the crime without persuasion from the undercover officer.

In one Canadian case where entrapment was argued, the accused obtained a stay of proceedings on the ground that he was induced by an undercover RCMP officer to commit the offence. The court found the accused would not have committed the offence without persuasion from the agent.

The courts have power to stay proceedings in oppressive cases which amount to an abuse of process. Judges could apply this power to all cases of illegally obtained evidence. It could be a solution to violation of arrest, search, and seizure laws by police.

The courts are concerned with the use of illegal police methods to obtain confessions. Where a confession is alleged, the court holds a hearing within the trial to determine whether the statement was voluntary. A confession obtained under pressure or threat, or in response to a police promise, may be untrustworthy. If you confess from the fear that the police are going to beat you, your confession is excluded.

The warning police should give to an accused person -- that he or she need not say anything in reply to the charge, but that anything he or she does say can be given in evidence against him or her -- has an unclear position in Canadian law. Judges look carefully at the circumstances of a confession by an accused who wasn't warned. However, the warning isn't mandatory. It should be made an ingredient of lawful arrest.

POSTSCRIPT THREE

WHAT TO DO IN THE EVENT OF
POLICE MISCONDUCT

We have mentioned the possibility of bringing action against the police for illegal actions. Police misconduct can be remedied by suing the offending officer for damages in a civil court, or by laying a criminal charge against him or her, or both.

...I am not obliged to submit to a search unless I am under arrest. I must warn you that any attempt on your part to violate my right to be free from arbitrary search may lead to a civil suit against you for damages etc..etc...

In these proceedings it is desirable for you to have witnesses. If you witness a person being assaulted by a police officer, stay and watch. Volunteer to give evidence in an action against the police officer.

Suppose a constable asks you to come to the station without legally arresting you. You ask what the charge is and he or she refuses to state one. You are entitled to resist. If you are then forcibly taken to the station, you can sue civilly for assault, battery (if you are struck), false arrest, and false imprisonment.

In civil court you must start an action by issuing a writ. You will need a lawyer. It is impossible for a layperson to start and prosecute such proceedings to a conclusion without the assistance of competent counsel.

An assault is any touching of your person without your consent. An assault may be by threat. If the officer indicates that he or she is going to use force, assault is complete. Your co-operation, on the basis that you don't want to get punched, is not consent.

False imprisonment is complete deprivation of liberty for any time, however short, without lawful cause. The restraint may result from actual physical force amounting to an assault or from fear that force will be used. Anyone who helps to continue the wrongful detention is party to it.

If someone maliciously charges you with an offence and there is no evidence to support the charge, you may have an action for damages for malicious prosecution. Malice can be proved by showing that the real intention was to injure you rather than to seek justice. You can sue the person who started the proceedings against you and anyone else who had a part in your being prosecuted.

In one successful suit, a twenty-year-old youth sued two police officers for assault and false imprisonment. Shortly after midnight one night the plaintiff and a friend were walking toward the friend's home. Two plainclothes officers in a marked police car stopped them. One officer asked for identification, but the plaintiff refused and asked the officer to identify himself first. The officer produced a badge but wouldn't give his name. The plaintiff again refused to identify himself. A scuffle ensued and the plaintiff was injured. The officers forced him into the police car and took him to the station. He wasn't given any reason for the arrest.

Police testified they stopped the two young men because they were sauntering along the street and because of their attire which the court found was not particularly distinctive. There had been break-ins in the neighborhood a few nights before and it was reported a person wearing rubber-soled shoes was involved. The plaintiff's companion was wearing rubber-soled shoes.

The court found the police had no reasonable and probable grounds to believe the plaintiff had committed or was about to commit an indictable offence and there were no vagrancy circumstances. They could ask, but not compel, him to identify himself. He was entitled to know whether he was under arrest and on what charge. He did not have to submit to imprisonment unless he knew the reason for it. He was entitled to resist. The plaintiff recovered damages and court costs.

A charge of common assault can be laid against an officer who illegally arrests or searches you without your consent. A charge of breaking and entering can be laid if police break into your house without a warrant.

Theft charge can be laid if they take anything without lawful authority. A charge of mischief can be laid if they cause damage without lawful justification. If an officer tells lies at your trial, lay a charge of perjury.

You have a right to lay a charge against a police officer who commits an offence. The first step is to attend before a justice of the peace. Tell the J.P. you wish to swear an information alleging an assault by a police officer and give the officer's name. If you have only a badge number, get the name from the Chief of Police. The J.P. may interview you and your witnesses. He or she may be reluctant to deal with the matter and direct you to speak with the prosecutor.

Insist that the charge be laid. If it is refused, you should complain to the Attorney-General or justice minister in your province. You can do this by writing an open letter to the Attorney-General, giving copies of it to your local newspapers. You could also start a petition, gather a large number of signatures, and send it to the Attorney-General.

It may be more effective to go to the office of the Attorney-General in person to protest refusal to lay the charge. This might attract greater publicity. Public opinion is sometimes the best weapon against public officials who deny you your rights.

POSTSCRIPT FOUR

WAR MEASURES ACT

It is important to realize that all the liberties which are guaranteed in the Bill of Rights and all the rules regarding lawful arrest, search, and seizure are not relevant in a situation where the War Measures Act has been invoked. The War Measures Act, when it comes into effect, expressly arrests the operation of the Bill of Rights. Parliament, by using the War Measures Act, can create new offences, change the laws of arrest, search, seizure, bail, trial, and sentence and do anything incidental to achieve its purpose.

ORDER FORM

FOR SELF-COUNSEL SERIES

Quantity		Price
	NATIONAL TITLES	
....	CANADIAN BOATING LAW	$2.95
....	CANADIAN CONSUMER HANDBOOK	$2.95
....	CANADIAN CREDIT LAW HANDBOOK	$2.95
....	CANADIAN GUIDE TO DEATH AND DYING	$3.50
....	CANADIAN INCOME TAX	$2.95
....	CIVIL RIGHTS IN CANADA	$2.50
....	GUIDE TO STARTING A SUCCESSFUL BUSINESS	$2.95
....	HOW TO IMMIGRATE INTO CANADA	$2.95
....	HOW TO SURVIVE RETIREMENT IN CANADA	$3.50
....	MENTAL PATIENTS AND THE LAW	$2.95
....	OUR ACCOUNTANT'S GUIDE TO RUNNING A SMALL BUSINESS	$2.95
....	SUCCESSFUL JOB-HUNTING	$1.95

PROVINCIAL TITLES

Please indicate which provincial edition is required.

		Price
....	FAMILY LAW AND GUIDE TO DRAFTING MARRIAGE CONTRACTS ☐ British Columbia	$3.50
....	DIVORCE GUIDE ☐ Ontario $7.95 ☐ British Columbia ☐ Alberta $6.95	$6.95
....	EMPLOYEE/EMPLOYER RIGHTS ☐ Ontario $1.95 ☐ British Columbia	$2.95

.... FIGHT THAT TICKET
    ☐ Ontario $2.50   ☐ Alberta $1.95
    ☐ British Columbia $1.95

.... INCORPORATION GUIDE $9.95
    ☐ Ontario   ☐ British Columbia   ☐ Alberta

.... LANDLORD/TENANT RELATIONS
    ☐ Ontario $2.50   ☐ British Columbia $2.50
    ☐ Alberta $2.50

.... REAL ESTATE GUIDE
    ☐ Ontario $3.50   ☐ British Columbia $3.50
    ☐ Alberta $3.95

.... LAYMAN'S GUIDE TO DRAFTING WILLS/
PROBATE PROCEDURE $2.95
    ☐ Ontario   ☐ Alberta   ☐ British Columbia

.... GUIDE TO SMALL CLAIMS COURT
    ☐ Ontario $2.95   ☐ British Columbia $2.95
    ☐ Alberta $2.95

.... PROBATE GUIDE $9.95
    ☐ British Columbia

Prices subject to change without notice.

Cheque or Money Order enclosed.

NAME ....

ADDRESS ....

CITY .... PROVINCE ....

If order is under $6.00, add 20¢ for postage and handling.

Please send orders from Manitoba, Saskatchewan, Alberta, British Columbia, Yukon Territory, or Northwest Territories to:

    INTERNATIONAL SELF-COUNSEL PRESS LTD.
    Head & Editorial Office:
    306 West 25th Street,
    North Vancouver, B.C.
    Phone (604) 987-2412

Please send orders from Ontario, Quebec, Nova Scotia, New Brunswick, Prince Edward Island, or Newfoundland to:

    SELF-COUNSEL DISTRIBUTORS LTD.
    R.R. #1,
    Pefferlaw, Ontario.
    Phone (705) 437-2565

FOR CASE LAW STUDY SERIES

Presenting all new, revised and up-dated low cost Canadian legal reference material for the law student, library or anyone else with more than a casual interest in law.

Quantity	Title	Price
....	A.B.C. OF EVIDENCE	$3.95
....	COMMERCIAL LAW	$3.95
....	COMPANY LAW	$3.95
....	CONSTITUTIONAL LAW	$4.95
....	CONTRACTS	$5.95
....	CREDITOR'S REMEDIES	$3.95
....	CRIMINAL LAW	$4.95
....	CRIMINAL PROCEDURE	$5.95
....	EVIDENCE	$4.95
....	FAMILY LAW	$7.95
....	INCOME TAX	$6.95
....	REAL PROPERTY	$5.95
....	TORTS	$4.95
....	TRUSTS	$4.95

Prices subject to change without notice.

Cheque or Money Order enclosed.

Name .... Order No. ....

Address .... Date ....

City .... Zone .... Province ....

If order is under $6.00, add 20¢ for postage and handling.